Quick Guide

WINDOWS & DOORS

CREATIVE HOMEOWNER PRESS®

COPYRIGHT © 1994
CREATIVE HOMEOWNER PRESS®
A Division of Federal Marketing Corp.
Upper Saddle River, NJ

Manufactured in the United States of America

Technical Editor: Mark Feirer
Cover Design: Warren Ramezzana
Cover Illustrations: Moffit Cecil
Book Packager: Scharff Limited
Printed at: Quebecor Printing Inc.

Current Printing (last digit)
10 9 8 7 6 5 4 3 2

Quick Guide: Windows & Doors
LC: 93-71659
ISBN: 1-880029-23-5

CREATIVE HOMEOWNER PRESS®
A Division of Federal Marketing Corp.
24 Park Way
Upper Saddle River, NJ 07458

C O N T E N T S

S A F E T Y   F I R S T

Though all the designs and methods in this book have been tested for safety, it is not possible to overstate the importance of using the safest construction methods possible. What follows are reminders; some do's and don'ts of basic carpentry. They are not substitutes for your own common sense.

■ *Always* use caution, care, and good judgment when following the procedures described in this book.

■ *Always* be sure that the electrical setup is safe; be sure that no circuit is overloaded, and that all power tools and electrical outlets are properly grounded. Do not use power tools in wet locations.

■ *Always* read container labels on paints, solvents, and other products. Provide proper ventilation, and observe all other warnings.

■ *Always* read the tool manufacturer's instructions for using a tool, especially the warnings.

■ *Always* use holders or pushers to work pieces shorter or more narrow than 3 inches on a table saw or jointer. Avoid working short pieces if you can.

■ *Always* remove the key from any drill chuck (portable or press) before starting the drill.

■ *Always* pay deliberate attention to how a tool works so that you can avoid being injured.

■ *Always* know the limitations of your tools. Do not try to force them to do what they were not designed to do.

■ *Always* make sure that any adjustment is locked before proceeding. For example, always check the rip fence on a table saw or the bevel adjustment on a portable saw before you start working on a project.

■ *Always* clamp small pieces firmly to a bench or other work surface when sawing or drilling.

■ *Always* wear the appropriate rubber or work gloves when handling chemicals, during heavy construction, or when sanding.

■ *Always* wear a disposable mask when working with odors, dusts, or mists. Use a special respirator when working with toxic substances.

■ *Always* wear eye protection, especially when using power tools or striking metal on metal or metal on concrete; a chip can fly off, for example, when chiseling concrete.

■ *Always* be aware that there is never time for your body's reflexes to save you from injury from a power tool in a dangerous situation. Everything happens too fast—be *alert!*

■ *Always* keep your hands away from the business ends of blades, cutters, and bits.

■ *Always* use a drill with an auxiliary handle to control the torque when large bits are used.

■ *Always* check your local building codes when planning new construction. The codes are intended to protect public safety—you should observe them to the letter.

■ *Never* work with power tools when you are tired or under the influence of alcohol or drugs.

■ *Never* cut very small pieces of wood or pipe. Cut only pieces large enough to clamp or hold securely.

■ *Never* change a blade or a bit unless the power cord is unplugged. Do not depend on the switch being off; you might accidentally hit it.

■ *Never* work in insufficient lighting.

■ *Never* work while wearing loose clothing, hanging hair, open cuffs, or jewelry.

■ *Never* work with dull tools. Have them professionally sharpened, or learn how to sharpen them yourself, using proper equipment.

■ *Never* use a power tool on a workpiece that is not firmly supported or clamped.

■ *Never* saw a workpiece that spans a large distance between horses without close support on either side of the kerf; the piece can bend, closing the kerf and jamming the blade, causing saw kickback.

■ *Never* support a workpiece with your leg or other part of your body when sawing.

■ *Never* carry sharp or pointed tools, such as utility knives, awls, or chisels in your pocket. If you want to carry tools, use a special-purpose tool belt with leather pockets and holders.

TOOL CHECKLIST

It is impossible to do good work without the proper tools and fasteners—and the knowledge of how to use them. Keep in mind that it is better to spend a little more money for quality; even the best carpenters cannot do good work with inferior tools.

Tools

You can build, install, and maintain windows, doors, and skylights with a modest set of tools. While the hand saw, keyhole saw, and other manual saws can do all the cutting, power saws are quicker. If you have a lot of trim work to do, a power miter saw is a good choice for doing the cutting. Be sure to follow all safety instructions when operating any power tools. Some tools, such as the sill-angle finder, are specialized and may be more difficult to locate; check the larger tool rental centers in your area.

Use any hammer you wish, but for delicate trim work a 10- or 12-ounce finishing hammer is better than the standard 16-ounce (or heavier) head. The lighter weight of the finishing hammer will give more control with the small finish nails typically used for trim.

A combination square is handy for marking exact 90-degree and 45-degree angles, and a try square can be used to check the work (such as a rough window opening) for square. Don't discount the value of a sharp pencil for marking measurements.

Finally, use the proper safety equipment: goggles, dust masks, and work gloves.

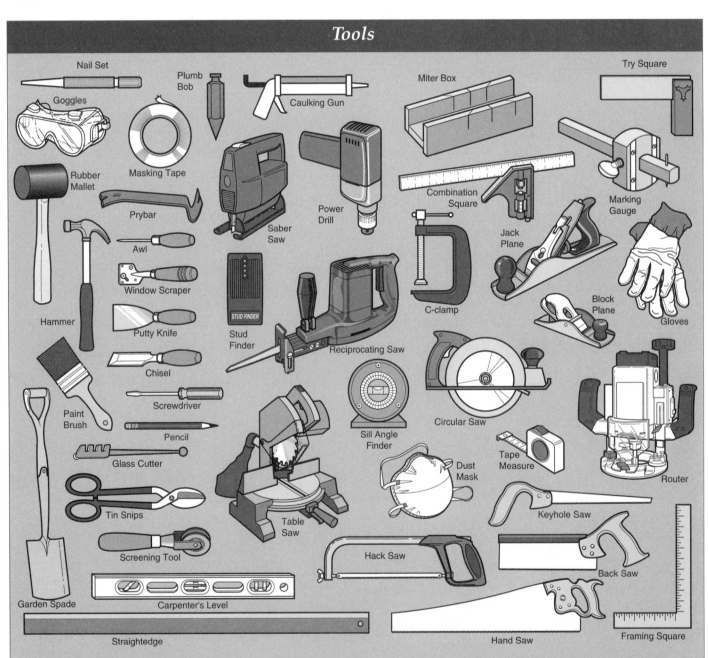

Tools

The tools and equipment shown above are essential for doing the various window, door, and skylight installation and repair projects discussed in this book.

Nails

Nails are usually sold by the pound, either from open stock or in packages. The price depends on several factors, including their material, coating (if any), design, and size. The length of a nail is indicated by its penny size; the letter designation for the word penny is the "d."

Hot-dipped galvanized nails are a good choice for installing windows, doors, and skylights. They are strong, durable, and, in the case of exterior use, corrosion-resistant. Fasteners made of cheaper materials can rust quickly and spoil the job. If the door or window is already painted the color you prefer, and you want to avoid having to fill the nail holes, use stainless steel ring-shank nails. Available at most lumberyards, these nails are more expensive, but well worth the added cost. Stainless steel ring-shank nails will not rust and cause streaks, and you don't have to countersink them. The heads are small, and the nails are available pre-painted, so you won't have to worry about touching them up. These nails are also a good choice if a clear finish is to be used.

For exterior applications, common and box nails are the best types to use because they hold well. Finishing nails are not generally recommended for outdoors because of their inferior holding power. Finishing nails are the best choice for trim work; be sure to use a size appropriate to the thickness of the casing.

For skylight flashing work, use nails made of material compatible with the metal. For example, copper flashing should be attached with only copper nails. When the flashing and nails are made from incompatible metals, galvanic corrosion will result, which can quickly eat away at the installation.

Nails should always be placed carefully so as to provide the greatest holding power. Placing nails too close to the edges of the wood will produce splitting. Avoid nailing into the end grain; if you must fasten into the end grain, use screws instead. When driving more than one nail, always stagger the nails so that none are in the same grain line. A few nails of the proper type and size, properly placed and driven, will hold better than a great many nails driven close together.

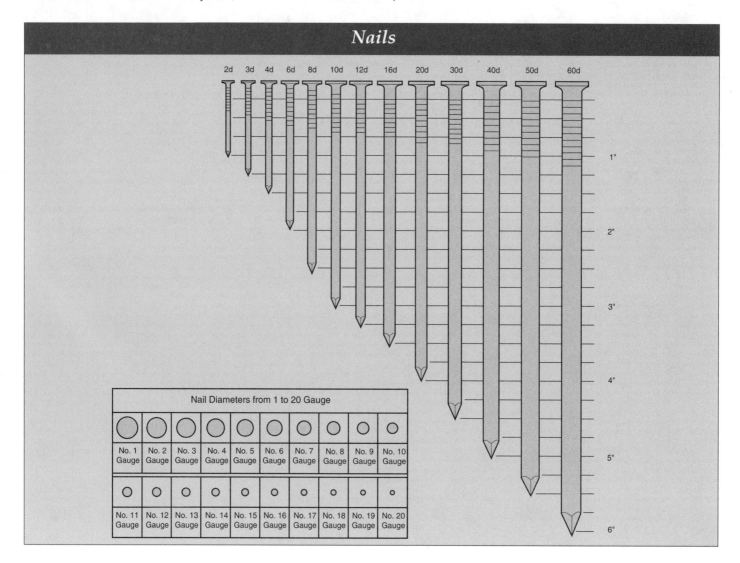

Nails

Nail Diameters from 1 to 20 Gauge

No. 1 Gauge	No. 2 Gauge	No. 3 Gauge	No. 4 Gauge	No. 5 Gauge	No. 6 Gauge	No. 7 Gauge	No. 8 Gauge	No. 9 Gauge	No. 10 Gauge
No. 11 Gauge	No. 12 Gauge	No. 13 Gauge	No. 14 Gauge	No. 15 Gauge	No. 16 Gauge	No. 17 Gauge	No. 18 Gauge	No. 19 Gauge	No. 20 Gauge

Screws

The number one consideration for screws when attaching door hinges and strike plates is strength. Steel wood screws are generally the strongest, but unless they are specially plated to resist rust, brass screws are better for outdoor use. Likewise, chrome- or nickel-plated screws are also ideal for exterior use.

Installation is made much easier if you first drill pilot screw holes. This has the added benefit of preventing the wood from splitting. Use of a screw-pilot bit in a power drill produces both a pilot hole to accommodate the screw threads and a countersink hole for the screw head.

Screws

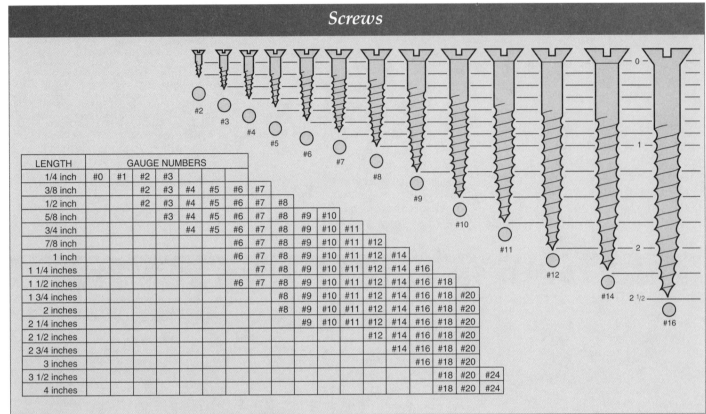

LENGTH	GAUGE NUMBERS																	
	#0	#1	#2	#3	#4	#5	#6	#7	#8	#9	#10	#11	#12	#14	#16	#18	#20	#24
1/4 inch	#0	#1	#2	#3														
3/8 inch			#2	#3	#4	#5	#6	#7										
1/2 inch			#2	#3	#4	#5	#6	#7	#8									
5/8 inch				#3	#4	#5	#6	#7	#8	#9	#10							
3/4 inch					#4	#5	#6	#7	#8	#9	#10	#11						
7/8 inch							#6	#7	#8	#9	#10	#11	#12					
1 inch							#6	#7	#8	#9	#10	#11	#12	#14				
1 1/4 inches								#7	#8	#9	#10	#11	#12	#14	#16			
1 1/2 inches							#6	#7	#8	#9	#10	#11	#12	#14	#16	#18		
1 3/4 inches									#8	#9	#10	#11	#12	#14	#16	#18	#20	
2 inches									#8	#9	#10	#11	#12	#14	#16	#18	#20	
2 1/4 inches										#9	#10	#11	#12	#14	#16	#18	#20	
2 1/2 inches													#12	#14	#16	#18	#20	
2 3/4 inches														#14	#16	#18	#20	
3 inches															#16	#18	#20	
3 1/2 inches																#18	#20	#24
4 inches																#18	#20	#24

Basic Procedures for Using Fasteners

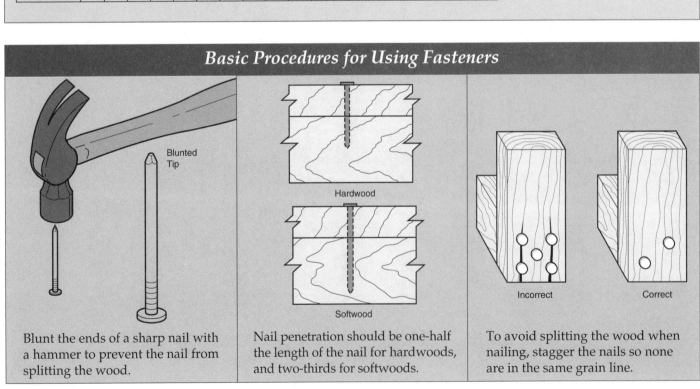

Blunt the ends of a sharp nail with a hammer to prevent the nail from splitting the wood.

Nail penetration should be one-half the length of the nail for hardwoods, and two-thirds for softwoods.

To avoid splitting the wood when nailing, stagger the nails so none are in the same grain line.

W I N D O W S

New windows can enhance the look, security, and energy efficiency of your home. A variety of window shapes, sizes, and features—and numerous decorative options, such as shutters and muntins—are available to complement the structure and motif of any room. They also provide the traditional functions of a window: To admit light and air and provide a view.

Types of Windows

There are five common types of windows. They can be used individually, or combined in various ways to achieve dramatic effects.

■ Fixed (or stationary) windows are the simplest type of window because they do not open. A fixed window is simply glass installed in a frame that is attached to the house. Such windows are the least expensive type, admit the mostlight, and come in the greatest variety of shapes and sizes. Unfortunately, they cannot be opened for ventilation.

■ Double-hung windows are perhaps the most common type used in houses. They consist of two framed glass panels that slide vertically, guided by a metal or wood track. One variation, called a single-hung window, consists of an upper panel that cannot slide and a lower, sliding panel. Cleaning the outside of a double-hung window can be awkward, though some new designs can be tilted inward for better access.

■ Casement windows are hinged at the side and swing outward from the window opening as you turn a small crank. Most importantly, they can be opened completely for maximum ventilation.

■ Awning windows generally swing outward like a casement window, but are hinged at the top. One feature of the window is that it can be left open slightly for ventilation even during light rain. One variation, called a hopper window, is hinged at the bottom and may open outward or inward.

■ Sliding windows are like a double-hung window turned on its side. The glass panels slide horizontally, and are often used where there is need for a window that is much wider than it is tall.

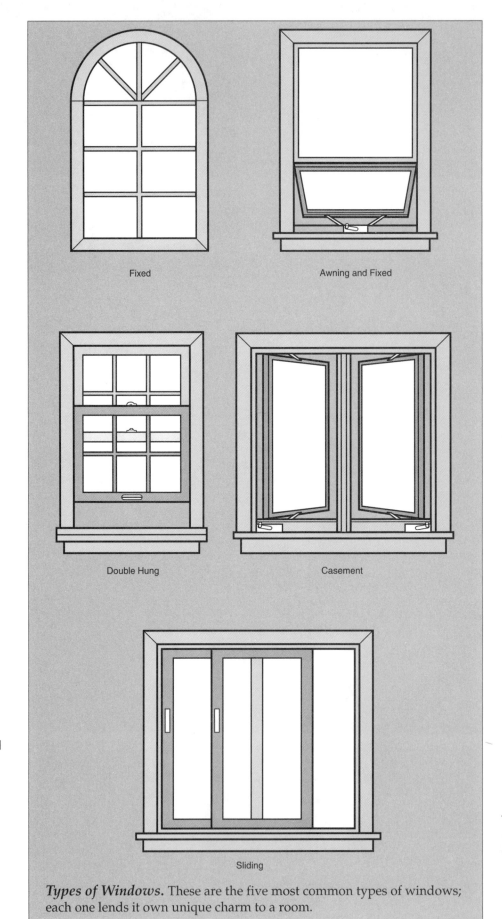

Fixed

Awning and Fixed

Double Hung

Casement

Sliding

Types of Windows. These are the five most common types of windows; each one lends it own unique charm to a room.

Window Features

If you had only to decide which of the five basic types of windows was right for your house, the job would be easy. But there are several other features to think about.

Glazing

As much as 30 percent of the energy lost from a house is lost through the windows. The kind of glass used in a window is perhaps the most important factor determining its energy-efficiency. Single-glazed windows are the least expensive, but are suitable only where energy loss is not a concern, such as a garage, or where protected by a storm window.

Double-glazed windows consist of two panes of glass separated by an airspace. The edges of such a window are sealed to prevent air between the panes from escaping; it is the air, and not the glass itself, that provides most of the insulating capability of the window. In very cold climates, triple-glazed windows may be cost effective.

High-performance glazing is becoming increasingly common, though it adds considerably to the cost of a window. In one version, a colorless gas replaces air between the panes. Because the gas is denser than air, it insulates better. Other versions, called low-emissivity

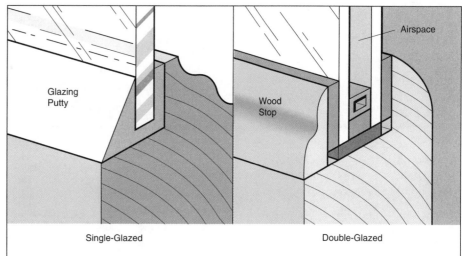

Glazing. Single-glazed windows have a single pane of glass that is held in place with glazing putty. Double-glazed windows have two panes of glass separated by an airspace. They are often held in place with wood stops.

(or "low-e") glazing, incorporate clear coatings or films that reduce the amount of heat radiated out through the glass.

Materials

The structural portions of a window are typically made of wood, but aluminum and extruded vinyl are also used. Wood improves the energy-efficiency of a window and is easy to work with. It must be painted or sealed, however, which makes it harder to maintain than vinyl or alu-minum. Some window manufacturers offer a composite window built of wood that is encased by vinyl. Often, the vinyl covers only the outside of the window, providing a wood interior you can paint or stain. These "clad" wood windows require little maintenance and are energy-efficient as well.

Hardware

The locks, hinges, and rotary operators available for windows come in various grades and several finishes. The quality of the hardware is one factor in the overall cost of the window.

Designing with Windows

For energy efficiency, place windows where they can take greatest advantage of the sun's heat and light and where they can be opened for natural cross ventilation. Here are some tips to keep in mind:

■ For the most light, use one large window, rather than several smaller ones. To get even light throughout the room, use windows in more than one wall. Tall windows let light farther into the room than short, wide ones.

■ For good ventilation, the size of the window openings should equal at least 10 percent of each room's floor area. Windows on opposite walls are best; adjacent walls, next best.

■ For the most energy savings, keep the sun in mind. Where winters are cold, the largest window areas should face south to take advantage of solar gain. The smallest amount of glass should be on the north side. Where air conditioning costs are a prime concern, the largest window area should be to the north and the smallest to the west and south.

Anatomy of a Window

The basic components of all windows have the same names, but because some windows are mechanically simpler than others, not all have a full range of parts. The following components can be found on a standard double-hung window, the most complicated type and one of the most common.

■ The sash is the framework into which the glass is set. Double-hung windows have two sash.

■ Strips called muntins separate the panes. In older windows, muntins hold the glass in place; on newer windows, they may simply be decorative. In some new models, muntins also called grilles, can be removed.

■ Jambs form the frame in which the sash slides. The top, horizontal jamb is called the head jamb; it is connected to side jambs. Concealed behind the side jambs on old double-hung windows are heavy metal sash weights connected to the sash with rope-and-pulley systems. The weights provide a counterbalance that makes the sash easier to open. Newer windows use a revolving drum in the head jamb or tubed tension springs in the side jambs instead of sash weights.

■ A series of stops attached to the jambs provides channels in which the sash can slide. Blind stops are permanently attached to the outside edges of the jambs, but both a parting stop (separating the two sash) and an inside stop can be pried loose to remove the sash.

■ A sash lock squeezes the sash together, keeping the window securely closed and minimizing drafts where the sash meet.

■ Interior casing at the sides and top and an apron across the bottom cover gaps between jambs and walls.

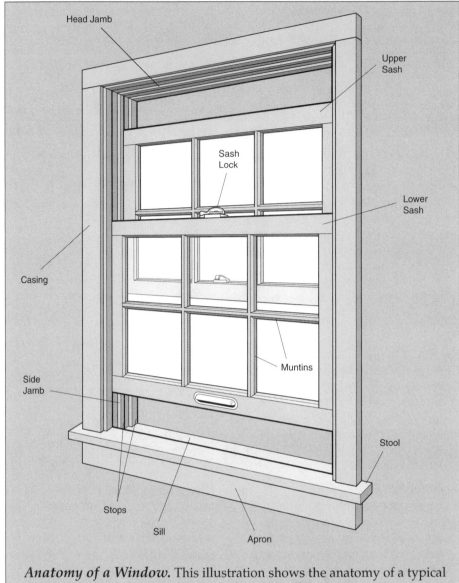

Anatomy of a Window. This illustration shows the anatomy of a typical double-hung window, as seen from the inside of the house.

■ The lower sash comes to rest behind a flat stool or interior sill; its outside counterpart, the exterior sill, is sloped so water will run off.

■ Weatherstripping (not shown here) is used to keep air from leaking around the sash when the window is closed. It may consist of flexible strips of plastic or brass, compressible foam, or vinyl gaskets.

Double-hung windows come as assembled units, except for the casing, apron, and (sometimes) the stool. These pieces are usually cut and fitted after the window is installed in the rough opening.

The position of a window in a wall is also related to the use of the room. Rooms in which people generally sit—dining rooms, for example—tend to have lower windows. Kitchen windows must be high enough to leave room for base cabinets. In bedrooms, windows should allow room for typical bedroom furniture. Building codes require, however, that at least one window in every bedroom be low and large enough so it can be used for escape in case a fire blocks other escape routes. Check your local codes for requirements.

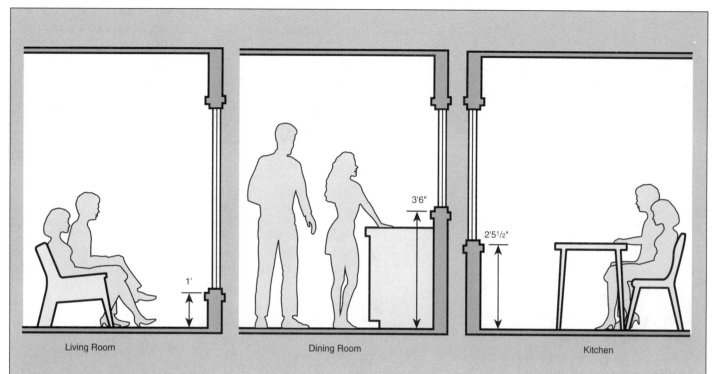

Living Room   Dining Room   Kitchen

Window Placement. The top of a window is typically placed at the same level as the top of a door. This is not required, but usually looks best.

Installation Basics

Installation techniques vary according to the type of window, but all windows fit within an opening in the wall framing called a rough opening. The rough opening is slightly bigger than the overall dimensions of the window unit so the unit can be plumbed and leveled as needed. A header sets at the top of the opening and supports the weight of the house above. Trimmer studs support the header.

Windows may be installed within the rough opening in several ways. Most windows are nailed either through the jambs or through the casing, and into the framing surrounding the rough opening. Metal, vinyl, and clad wood windows are usually nailed to the sheathing of a house through a perforated flange surrounding the window. This makes them easier to install than other types of windows.

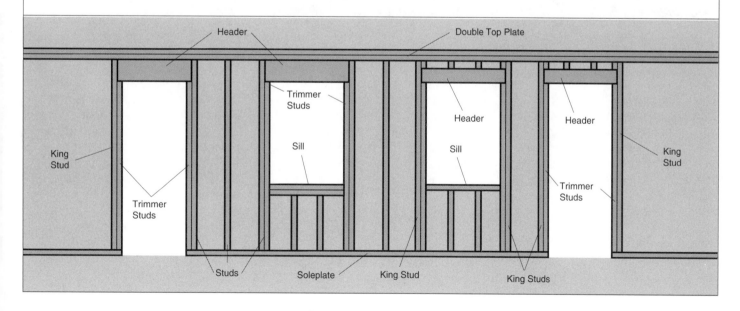

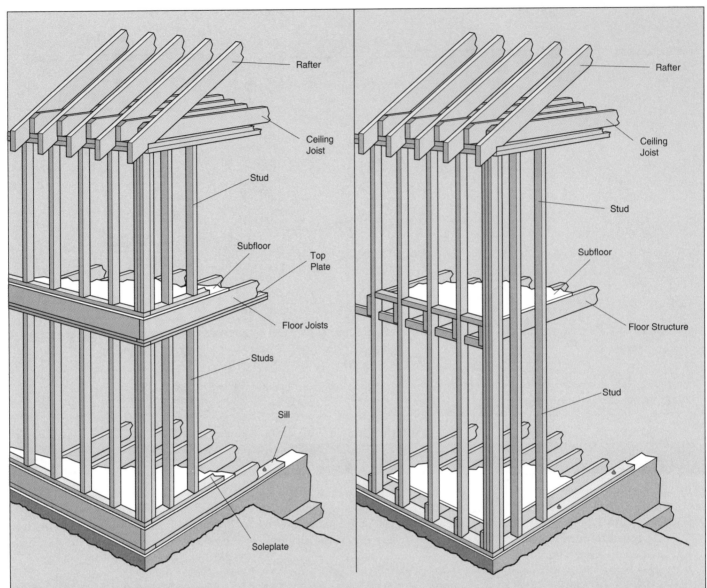

Anatomy of a Wall. Platform framing (left) looks like this two-story example. It requires many relatively short pieces of lumber and is built in layers. Balloon-framed houses (right) are rarely built these days. The technique requires unusually long wall studs, which are no longer readily available.

Anatomy of a Wall

If your house is built of wood, as opposed to masonry, you have a wide selection of windows from which to choose. Though the exact type of wood construction has little bearing on how a window is actually installed, you still should know a little about how your walls are built. The information will be particularly useful if you plan to install a window where there was none before, or if you want to replace a small window with a larger one. Be aware, though, that any opening cut in an exterior wall can affect the structural integrity of a house. If you have any doubt about your ability to do the work properly, get help from a builder or contractor.

Conventional Framing

By far the most common type of house construction consists of many many pieces of lumber—studs, rafters, and joists—that are nailed together into a rigid framework. This framework, or framing, is the skeleton of a house. The sheathing consists of plywood or some other panel product (nailed to the framing) and siding (nailed to the plywood). Platform framing is the type of framing used on most houses built these days. The floor structure forms a "platform" upon which the walls are framed. Balloon framing is rarely used today, but you might encounter it in old houses. It consists of long pieces of lumber that reach from foundation to roof.

Masonry Construction

In several parts of the country, houses are commonly built with bricks or masonry blocks instead of wood framing. All the basic types of windows are available for masonry houses, though specific installation details vary. As for windows, the main difference from wood frame construction is that with masonry construction it is much more difficult to add a new window or enlarge an old one.

Timber Framing

Some new houses, particularly in the Northeast, Northwest and Upper Midwest, have been built using a very old construction technique. Instead of assembling walls using many small pieces of dimension lumber, builders of these houses use relatively few 8 inch by 8 inch (or larger) wood timbers. And instead of being nailed together, the timbers are connected with wood pegs or by interlocking joinery.

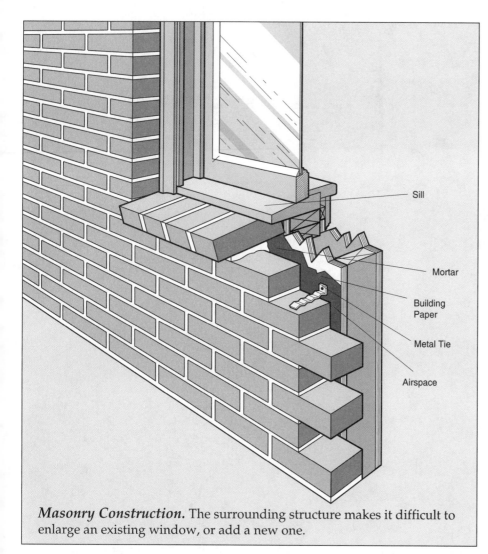

Sill

Mortar

Building Paper

Metal Tie

Airspace

Masonry Construction. The surrounding structure makes it difficult to enlarge an existing window, or add a new one.

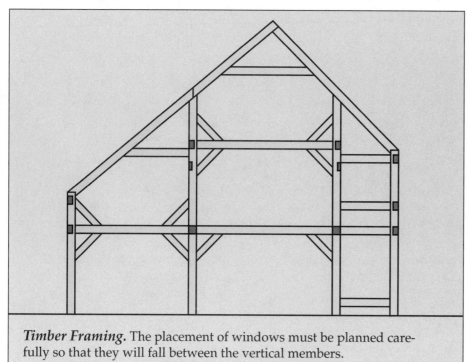

Timber Framing. The placement of windows must be planned carefully so that they will fall between the vertical members.

Installing Sash Replacement Kits

Sometimes a window can be improved considerably without replacing the entire unit. Several manufacturers make kits to replace just the sash, while keeping the jambs and the casing that are already in place. This option is particularly helpful if there is no need to change the size or location of the windows.

By replacing a single-glazed sash with a new double-glazed sash, the energy-efficiency will improve significantly. Along with the new sash, the kits include new tracks, called jamb liners, to hold the sash in place. The liners reduce air leakage around the sash, and also make it easier to raise and lower the windows. Another advantage of replacing just the sash is speed: the work goes quicker without removing the entire window unit first.

Measuring the Window. The most important step in the process is to measure existing windows carefully. The exact places to measure, and the tolerances, will vary from manufacturer to manufacturer, so decide on the brand of replacement sash before getting started. Generally, however, measure the width and height of the jambs (not including any stops), and the opening for any screens. It is usually helpful to make a sketch of

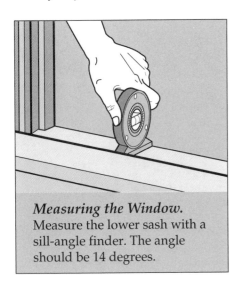

Measuring the Window. Measure the lower sash with a sill-angle finder. The angle should be 14 degrees.

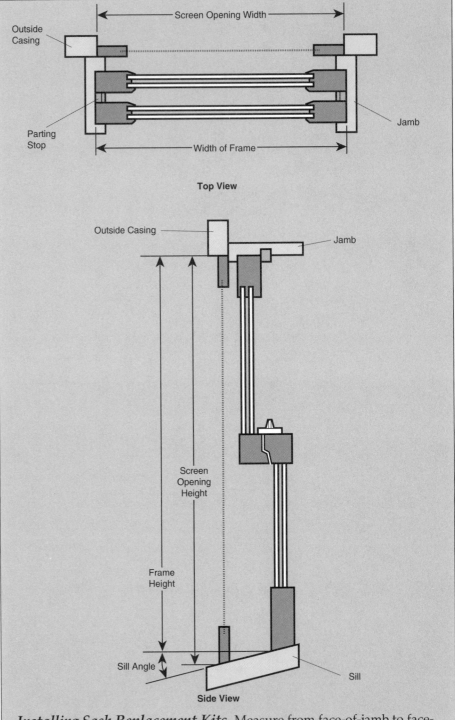

Top View

Side View

Installing Sash Replacement Kits. Measure from face-of-jamb to face-of-jamb, not from the stops. Height measurements should be taken from the points where the existing sash meets the jambs.

the window to show exactly where measurements were made.

It may also be necessary to measure the sill angle to ensure that the new lower sash seals properly against the sill. This measurement can be made with a sill-angle finder.

1 Removing the Sash and Stops. Before installing the new sash, remove the old sash and stops. Starting from the inside of the house, the order of removal is as follows: inside stop, lower sash, parting stop, and upper sash.

Depending on the window, it may be necessary to remove an outer stop. The stops can be pryed away from the jambs with a small prybar.

2 Installing the Jamb Liners.
With the old windows gone, install the jamb liners. If possible, screw them in place or use a special installation clip provided by the manufacturer. The liners are installed directly against both side jambs. They should fit snugly between head jamb and sill.

3 Installing the New Sash. The jamb liners are flexible enough so that the sash units can simply snap into place. First angle a sash into the opening, then level it out as shown. Finally lift the free end into position and push it against the jamb liner until the sash snaps into place. The sash can also be removed easily for cleaning simply by reversing this procedure.

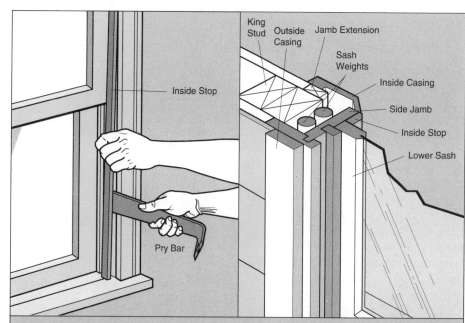

Inside Stop

King Stud
Outside Casing
Jamb Extension
Sash Weights
Inside Casing
Side Jamb
Inside Stop
Lower Sash

Pry Bar

1 Use a pry bar to remove the window stops one by one. No need to fill any of the nail holes because they will probably be covered by the new jamb liners, but it is necessary to scrape away any ridges of built-up paint that may interfere with proper placement of the liners.

Jamb Liner

2 If the bottoms of the liners are angled to match the sill, each kit will include a right-hand and a left-hand nailer.

Replacement Sash

3 Just snap the replacement sash in place. The sash can be painted before the installation. Be sure not to get paint on the sash edges because this will make the sash difficult to operate later on.

Removing Old Windows

If the entire window unit—jambs, sash, and casing—is going to be replaced, the first job is to remove the old unit. Because windows, particularly old ones, may have been installed in a variety of ways, consider the following tips simply as guidelines. In all cases, however, be careful when removing windows. The risk of breaking glass is one hazard, so run strips of tape across the glass to keep it from falling out if breakage occurs. Old windows commonly have layers upon layers of old paint, some of which are probably lead-based. Lead-based paint is now recognized as a health hazard, so wear a dust mask if you encounter flaking and peeling paint. Wear gloves, and remove any demolition debris promptly.

The technique for window removal will depend on the type of window. First, however, remove the interior and exterior casing and attached trim.

Wood Windows. Wood windows are nailed in place through the exterior casing or through the jambs. It is sometimes possible to cut through the nails holding jamb-nailed windows to the framing. Remove the casing and slice through the nails by reaching between jamb and framing with a hacksaw blade, or use a reciprocating saw fitted with a metal-cutting blade. In cases where the window has been nailed through the concealed portion of the blind stop, remove the exterior casing and pull any nails holding the window in place.

Steel Windows. Steel windows are generally screwed in place, so removing them involves a hunt for all the screws. If the windows are very old, screw heads may be concealed by layers of paint; and need to be scraped to find them.

Vinyl and Aluminum Windows. These are typically nailed to the sheathing through flanges, and can be difficult to remove gracefully.

Removing Old Windows. Window glass can break easily as the window is removed; tape will keep it from falling away from the window in dangerous shards. Windows are heavy, so enlist help to remove them.

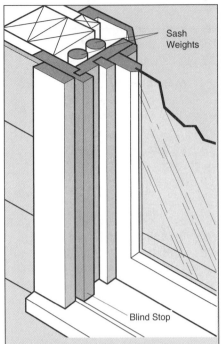

Wood Windows. Older windows with sash weights may be nailed directly to the framing. Remove the interior casing to gain access to the weights; remove the weights before working on the rest of the window.

Sash Weights

Blind Stop

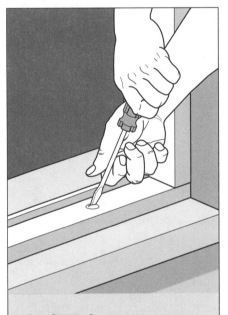

Steel Windows. If the screws holding steel windows have been painted over, clean the slots with a knife before using a screwdriver.

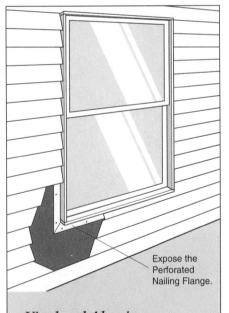

Vinyl and Aluminum Windows. To remove the nails holding a vinyl or aluminum window in place, remove some portion of the siding.

Expose the Perforated Nailing Flange.

Installing Replacement Windows

If replacing an existing window, save work by measuring carefully and ordering the new window to fit into the old rough opening. If you cannot find an exact replacement, a window that is slightly smaller than the old one will be easier to install than one that is slightly larger than the opening. To install wood replacement windows with integral casing or brick molding, follow these step-by-step instructions:

1 **Altering the Rough Opening.**
After removing the old window, check the measurements of the rough opening to see if the opening is square, plumb, and level. Minor problems can be dealt with by shimming the new window, but major problems should be corrected now. Add any additional framing to bring the opening to the proper size. In some cases you might need only to fill in at one side or another with a 1x4 or some 1/2-inch plywood. In either case, the stock should extend from rough sill to header.

2 **Installing the New Window.**
Unpack the new window and check it for square. If the manufacturer secured any braces or reinforcing blocks to the window, they should be left in place until the window has been nailed securely to the house. Some manufacturers recommend that the sash be removed before the installation of the window to prevent glass breakage, while others recommend leaving the sash in place to stiffen the jambs. Lift the window into place from the outside and have one person hold it firmly in place against the wall.

3 **Leveling the Window.** Check the sill for level. Shim beneath it as needed from inside the house. If the window is unusually wide, shim beneath the long sills as well. The sill

1 Check the rough opening in preparation for the new window. Fill in with new framing as necessary, and make sure any old nails have been removed or pounded flat.

2 Windows are heavy and fragile, so it helps to have two people to lift the window into place and steady it in the opening. Wood windows should be primed on all surfaces before installation.

Shims

Jamb Leg   Jamb Leg

3 With one person holding the window in place, check the sill for level and shim it as needed. Make sure the window is flat against the wall or you will not get accurate readings. Shims should be pieces of flat wood, not shingles, in order to provide full bearing to the jamb legs and intermediate supports.

should be checked frequently throughout the installation to ensure that it has not shifted out of position. Now pull the window away from the opening just enough to run a bead of exterior-grade caulk behind the casing and press the window against the wall.

4 **Setting the Window.** Secure one lower corner of the window to the wall by nailing through the casing with a 10d galvanized casing nail. A casing nail is similar to a finish nail, but its head has a slight flare to it and its shank is heavier than a finish nail of the same length.

Insert flashing over the head casing and slip it beneath the siding. If flashing was not included with the window, you can purchase it at a building supply store.

4 Do not set the nails completely until the window has been fully installed. The exposed head will make removal easier to adjust the position of the window.

5 **Plumbing the Window.** Now check the window for plumb. If the window was square when it was set into place and its sill was leveled, the jamb will be plumb. If it is not, double-check the sill. Check the window again for square and adjust it if necessary by slipping shim shingles between the jamb and the framing. Some people prefer to hold a level directly against the jamb instead of against the casing, just in case the two are not perfectly aligned. When the window is plumb, secure it with another nail.

6 **Nailing the Window.** Open and close the window to check its operation. If it binds, reposition the nails. If it works properly, however, complete the nailing. To secure the sill (it may not be nec-

5 When plumbing the window, a helper inside the house can insert shims as needed while you watch the level. If working alone, plumb and shim the jamb from inside the house. Be sure to nail through the casing near the top of the window to hold it in place.

essary with small windows), nail through the portion that is inside the house—nails in a sill exposed to weather may be a maintenance problem years from now. Be sure to nail through the shims or you may push the sill out of alignment.

7 **Caulking the Window.** Caulk the gap between the window casing and the siding with a high-quality exterior caulk. Don't forget to caulk any gaps beneath the sill.

8 **Insulating the Window.** Use a putty knife to stuff fiberglass insulation (don't pack it too hard) into the gaps between the window and the framing. Alternately, spray expanding foam sealant into the gaps. The window is now ready for interior casing.

6 Continue to nail through the casing, while checking the head jamb for level and the side jamb for plumb. Nails should be approximately 12 inches on center.

7 Caulk around the window except at the head flashing. Installed properly, the flashing will channel water away from the window; caulk might cause water to back up behind the siding.

8 Insulation prevents air infiltration around windows. If using fiberglass, wear gloves. Pack it loosely to aid its insulating properties. Use expanding foam sparingly; too much may push the jambs out of alignment as it expands.

Framing a New Window Opening

Installing a new window in a blank wall can transform the gloomiest room into a bright, airy space. Even a small window can do the trick. But for the project to be a success, plan carefully. Figure out precisely where to put the window, then cut a hole in the wall to accommodate it, add wood framing to provide a structure around it, and, finally, install it. The last step is the easiest—installing a window in a new opening is just like installing a replacement window (see page 19).

First, choose the size of window by consulting a manufacturer's catalog. It is less costly to choose a standard size window than it is to have the same manufacturer custom-build one. Then decide where the window will go and determine if there are any plumbing pipes, heating ducts, or electrical wires inside the wall. Wiring can be relocated easily, but pipes and ducts can be costly and time-consuming to move. Whenever possible, place the window to avoid them.

Here's a tip: Windows sometimes take a number of weeks to arrive after they have been ordered. Wait until the windows actually arrive before cutting open the wall. The actual dimensions of the window may not match the catalog dimensions exactly. Also, you won't have to spend weeks with a gaping hole in your wall.

The following method is just one way to frame a window opening in an existing wall, but it minimizes the amount of demolition (and subsequent repair) that you will have to do. As any professional remodeler knows, however, everything depends on what you find within the wall, and you never know that until you get there.

1 Finding Studs. After determining the approximate location of the window, find out exactly where the studs are in that portion of the wall. To do this pass a magnet over the wall to locate the vertical row of nails holding the drywall to each stud. Look for other clues, such as the location of wall outlets and switches—they are housed in metal or plastic boxes that are nailed to one side of a stud or the other. After finding one stud, it's easy to find others; they are usually 16 inches apart (measured from the centerline of one to the centerline of another).

2 Making the Rough Opening. Consult the manufacturer's catalog again to determine the size of the rough opening required for

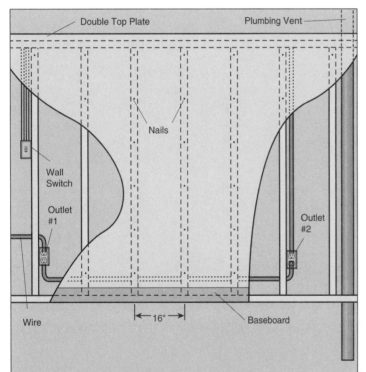

1 A window could be installed anywhere in the middle of this wall without much trouble because the wiring between outlets #1 and #2 need not be moved. If the window was centered in the right-hand portion of the wall, however, wiring extending upward from outlet #2 would have to be relocated and the plumbing vent might be in the way, too.

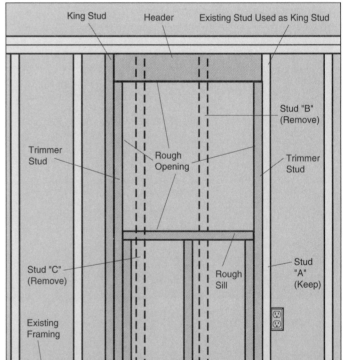

2 To minimize the cutting of existing studs, plan the new framing to take advantage of them. Here, existing stud "A" will serve as a king stud. Studs "B" and "C" are the only ones that will have to be removed. The window will rest on the rough sill.

the window. The opening will be slightly larger than the overall height and width of the window—about 5/8 inch wider and about 3/4 inch higher—to allow space for shimming the window. Using a long level or a plumb bob, mark two vertical lines on the wall that correspond to the inside edge of both trimmer studs; the lines should go from floor to ceiling. Then draw a horizontal line corresponding to the bottom of the header. The resulting lines will look something like a doorway; they indicate the minimum amount of drywall to remove. (You may have to remove drywall all the way up to the ceiling if you can't fit framing behind the drywall.)

3 **Removing the Drywall.** Use a keyhole saw to cut carefully along the layout lines—a circular saw will kick up too much dust, and by cutting with hand power instead of electrical power it's easier to stop before severing any unexpected wiring or plumbing lines. Do not cut through the soleplate or the double top plates, and do not cut through the wall sheathing and siding (you'll do that later). Cutting and removing drywall is messy work, so lay down a tarp to protect the floor.

4 **Removing the Old Insulation.** Take out all of the insulation between the studs, then remove the stud in the middle of the opening. It may be necessary to cut the stud out in sections because the top and bottom will be nailed to the plates, and the back edge will be pinned by nails driven through the sheathing. Pry out the stud pieces carefully.

5 **Constructing the Framing.** Start by cutting a king stud and a trimmer stud to fit (in this case) at the left-hand side of the rough opening; cut another trimmer for the right-hand side. Slip the king stud into place and toenail it to top and bottom plates. Remove a bit of drywall near the bottom of the king stud in order to reach it with a toenail, but the damage will be covered later with baseboard.

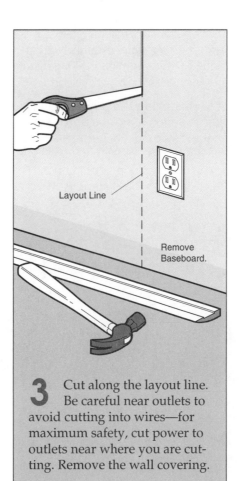

3 Cut along the layout line. Be careful near outlets to avoid cutting into wires—for maximum safety, cut power to outlets near where you are cutting. Remove the wall covering.

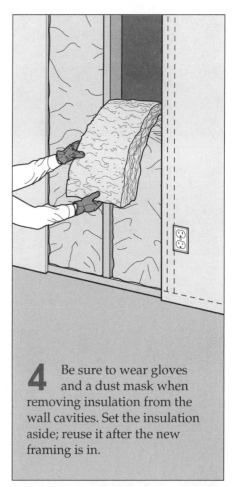

4 Be sure to wear gloves and a dust mask when removing insulation from the wall cavities. Set the insulation aside; reuse it after the new framing is in.

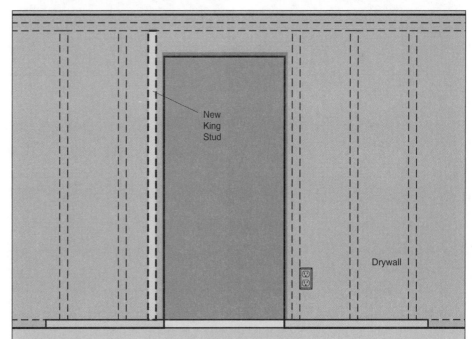

5 Maneuver the new king stud into place between the drywall and the backside of the sheathing. It should be about 1 1/2 inches in from the cut edge of the drywall. If you are unable to toenail it into the top of the stud, run a pair of long screws diagonally through the top of the stud and into the plate.

6 Building a Header. A header is a doubled framing member laid on edge over a window, door, or other opening to provide support for framing above the opening. To build a header, sandwich a length of 1/2-inch plywood between two knot-free two-by boards—the combined thickness will equal the thickness of a typical 2x4 wall.

In a nonbearing wall, use 2x6s. For a bearing wall, use the chart on page 55 to determine the dimension of the boards.

7 Installing the Header. Lift the header into place against the underside of the top plate and have a helper hold it there while you toenail it into place at both ends. After finishing this, slip both trimmer

studs into place to support the header. Nail them into the king studs with a 10d nail every 16 inches or so.

8 Completing the Framing. Add the rough sill and the cripple studs to support it. Nail down through the sill and into the ends of the cripple studs with 16d nails; use 10d nails for the rest of the nailing. Nail the loose edges of the drywall to the window framing as needed, using drywall nails. Fill in above and below the window with new drywall. (Don't forget to insulate before piecing in the drywall.)

9 Cutting the Sheathing and Siding. Use a hand saw from inside the house to cut along the lines defined by the rough opening. A quicker way is to cut from the outside using a circular saw or reciprocating saw. To do this, drill a small hole through the sheathing at each corner of the rough opening, and stick a nail through each one to

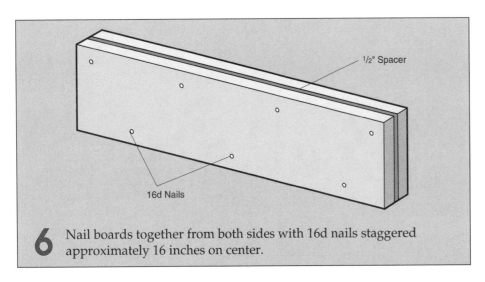

6 Nail boards together from both sides with 16d nails staggered approximately 16 inches on center.

7 The header can be toe-nailed to the king studs with 10d nails, then supported with trimmer studs. It may be necessary to remove dry-wall up to the ceiling to fit in the header.

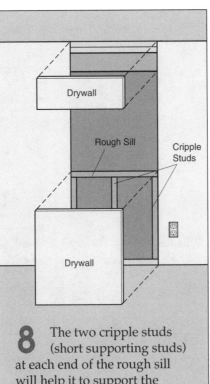

8 The two cripple studs (short supporting studs) at each end of the rough sill will help it to support the weight of the window, but they also serve as a nailing base for the attachment of drywall.

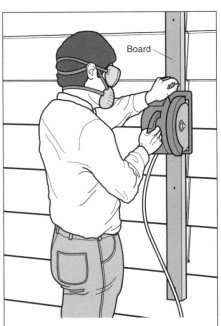

9 When using a circular saw, the base bumps into the edges of the siding while cutting vertically. Instead, tack a board to the siding. Set the depth of the blade, and guide the saw while sliding it on the board.

find them from outside; connect the corners, remove the nails, and cut along the lines.

10 **Removing Siding for Casing.** Cut away a bit more of the siding to provide bearing for the casing (or nailing flange) of the window. Have a helper hold the window in the rough opening while leveling the window. Then trace around the casing and remove the window. Set the saw to cut through the siding (but not the sheathing) along the layout lines. With this portion of the siding removed, the window will fit flat against the sheathing.

11 **Installing the Window.** Use the same approach that was used earlier for installing a replacement window. Caulk gaps between the casing and the siding.

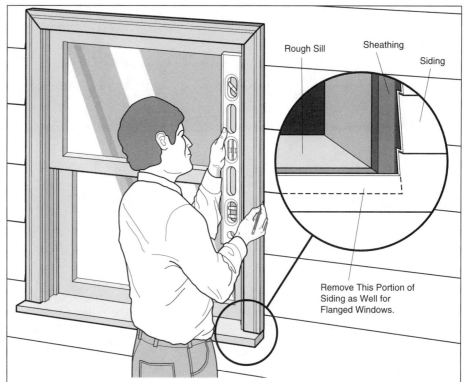

Rough Sill

Sheathing

Siding

Remove This Portion of Siding as Well for Flanged Windows.

10 If the window has a nailing flange, you'll have to remove a portion of the siding along the bottom of the rough opening in addition to the portion removed along head and side jambs.

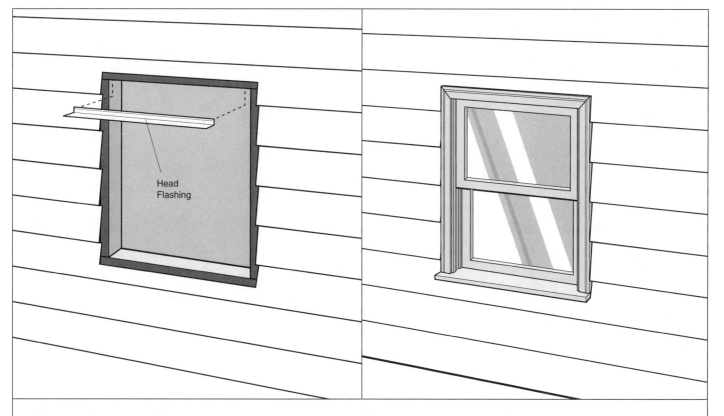

Head Flashing

11 Slip the head flashing into place with one leg extended beneath the siding. Plumb and install the window by nailing through the shims or the sill could be pushed out of alignment.

Details for Siding

Whenever cutting into a wall in preparation for adding a window, you'll have to deal with one type of siding or another. Cutting through the various sidings is not difficult in itself. What takes time and thought is making sure that you have left no avenues by which water can get into the walls. Even a minor leak could lead to major structural problems over time. For a good idea of how to handle the details around a window, take a close look at some of the existing windows to see how the siding was handled.

Typically, not much siding is needed when filling in around a window or door. In fact, it's possible to have enough using the siding already removed—if it was removed carefully. It's always a good idea to set aside any materials removed during the job, keeping them on hand until all work is done. If your house is old, it's even more important to salvage as much as possible because matching siding may no longer be available. If it is necessary to purchase additional siding, take a piece of the old existing siding to the lumberyard to get the closest possible match.

Wood Bevel Siding

Also called clapboard siding, this material comes in wedge-shaped lengths that are applied horizontally. Each course of siding overlaps the course below it to keep water out. Nails are placed so that they will be covered by successive courses of siding. To apply lap siding, start at the bottom of the wall and work upward, matching existing courses as you go. Nail with 6d or 8d galvanized siding nails. Seams between boards in each course should be staggered.

Vinyl and Aluminum Siding

These sidings depend on interlocking joints to keep water out. Installation recommendations vary

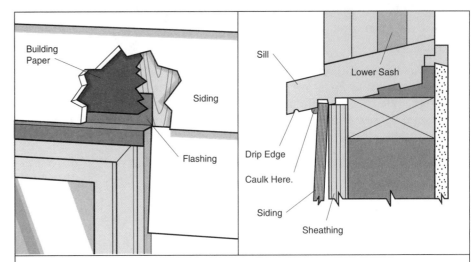

Wood Bevel Siding. The head of a window is protected by metal flashing that slips beneath wood bevel siding and laps over the top of the window (left). The siding should not rest directly on the flashing; a small gap will allow water to drain away freely. Lap siding slips into a groove cut in the underside of the window sill (right). This joint should also be caulked. The smaller groove in the front edge of the sill is a drip edge; it prevents water flowing over the sill from continuing back to the siding.

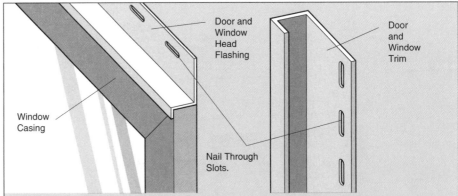

Vinyl and Aluminum Siding. Vinyl and aluminum siding details vary by manufacturer, but various trim pieces such as these are generally required around windows and doors.

according to the manufacturer, but one general nailing tip is to avoid driving nails hard against the siding's nailing flange. The siding expands and contracts considerably, and nails must allow for this movement.

Wood Shingle Siding

Wood shingles come in 16-, 18-, and 24-inch lengths, and in random widths. The key to installing shingles is to be sure that the gaps between shingles in a course do not line up with gaps in the two courses below. The installation of shingles varies

considerably from region to region, so your best guide is to ask for installation tips from home center personnel and local professionals.

Plywood Siding

The siding should be cut so that it fits closely against the window. Sometimes the window casing will actually fit over the siding. In such cases, the window should be bedded in a bead of caulk during installation. As with other sidings, install galvanized metal head flashing above the window.

Installing Flanged Windows

At one time, the only windows with a perimeter nailing flange were metal windows. Now, however, there is a flange on windows made of aluminum, vinyl, and vinyl-covered wood (clad windows). Small greenhouse windows are another type of flanged window, and may be installed in a similar fashion (large greenhouse windows may require special detailing, however; refer to manufacturer's instructions). Rough openings for all flanged windows are typically smaller than they would be for a standard window of the same size. This is because there is no need to shim the sides of the window. That makes installation easy. The following steps detail the basic installation steps, but always defer to the instructions included with your window because details vary according to the manufacturer.

1 **Making the Rough Opening.** If putting in a window where there wasn't one before, consult the manufacturer's literature to determine the dimensions of the rough opening. Once the framing is complete, nail the sheathing into place. If installing a flanged window in an existing opening, you may have to cut the siding back slightly to accommodate the flanges. In either case, place the window into the rough opening.

2 **Leveling the Sill.** Check the sill for level, and shim beneath the window from inside the house as necessary. Begin nailing the window into place on one side, using 1 3/4-inch roofing nails through existing slots in the flange.

3 **Nailing the Window.** Nail through the flange on the other side of the window, checking for plumb. The best technique is to drive the first few nails partway, fully driving them home only after you're sure the window is plumb and level. After several nails are in place, check the operation of the window by opening and closing it several times.

4 **Finishing the Window.** Install trim or replace the siding around the window as needed to match the other windows of the house. The casing should fit snugly between the edges of the siding and the side of the window. Caulk inboth places. If head flashing was supplied with the window, go ahead and install it now.

1 As you set the window into place, run a generous bead of caulk between the flange and the sheathing.

2 Place nails at each corner, at least every 10 inches around the window.

3 Drive nails halfway, then check for plumb.

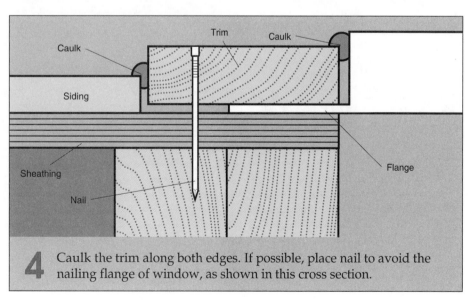

4 Caulk the trim along both edges. If possible, place nail to avoid the nailing flange of window, as shown in this cross section.

Jamb Extensions

In order for interior and exterior trim to fit properly, the jambs of a window must match the thickness of the wall. Generally this isn't much of a problem because walls of most newer houses are a standard thickness. There's more variation in older houses, however. Custom windows can be built to fit the thickness of the walls, but it is very expensive. You might be able to plane down the jambs of windows that are slightly too wide for the wall. But the easiest and most common solution to this problem is to buy windows with jambs that are thinner than the walls and then fit the windows with jamb extensions.

Jamb extensions are wood strips nailed to the indoor edges of the jambs to make up the difference in thickness between jamb and wall. When ordering windows, order the jamb extensions at the same time, or make your own with a table saw. If planning to stain or use a clear finish on the jambs and trim, the jamb extensions should be made of the same wood as the windows. If painting everything, be sure to use an inexpensive and easy-to-work wood, such as pine, for the extensions. Just be sure that whatever wood you use is straight and relatively clear. Because jamb extensions are so slender, any knots will make them too fragile to work with.

Making & Installing Jamb Extensions

Jamb extensions are added after installing the window, and making them is easy with a table saw. Using this tool will ensure that the jamb extensions are cut to a uniform dimension. Caution: whenever cutting wood into thin strips, use a push stick or some other method to keep fingers well away from the saw blade.

1 Cutting the Boards. Start with a board that is at least as long as the longest length of jamb extension. Set the table saw and simply rip the board repeatedly.

2 Marking the Inward Facing Surface. Spread all the pieces out on a table so each side that will face inward (toward the window) faces up. The inward facing surface will be the most visible after installation, so now's the time to select it. Then line up all the strips and draw a pencil line across them. While installing the strips, look for the pencil line—no need to think about which side faces where.

3 Completing the Jamb Extensions. Cut the extensions to length. Use a simple butt joint—not a miter—because casing will later cover most of the joint anyway. Nail the extensions to the window jambs with finish nails.

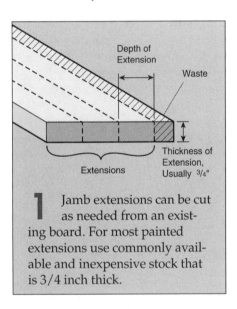

1 Jamb extensions can be cut as needed from an existing board. For most painted extensions use commonly available and inexpensive stock that is 3/4 inch thick.

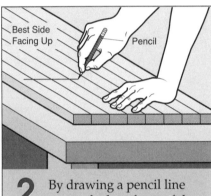

2 By drawing a pencil line across the best faces of the cut jamb extensions, there's little chance of accidentally installing them improperly.

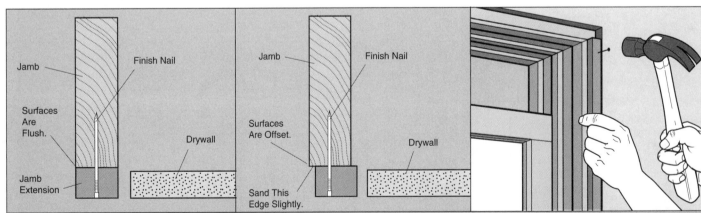

3 Jamb extensions are sometimes installed so the inner face is flush with the surface of the jamb, but can also be offset slightly. If offset, round off the sharp edges of the jamb before installing the extensions; paint holds better to slightly rounded edges. Finish nails used to attach jamb extensions should be long enough to penetrate about 1 inch into the jamb.

Customizing Windows

Windows can complement a decorating motif in a room on the inside of a home as well as add to the architectural style of the exterior. Many traditional looks rely upon muntins, shutters, semicircular fanlights, and assorted moldings for continuity in design and visual interest. Look through the millwork catalog at a well-stocked lumberyard to find a wide array of window dressings. One or a combination of these components can give windows a custom look.

Muntins. Years ago, when window glass was weaker, muntins, or small framing members that divided the panes of glass in a sash, served to bind individual panes together. Muntins are no longer needed for strength, but yesterday's charm is almost instantly attainable by using snap-in muntin grilles. They are available for windows of various sizes and shapes, and should be ordered with the window.

Snap-In Style. Ready-made rectangular and diamond configurations give the same overall effect as the originals, with the added benefit of easy removal for cleaning. For standard-sized, newer windows, check with a local dealer for snap-in units. For windows that are older or an unusual size, muntin grilles may have to be custom-made.

Shutters. Exterior or interior shutters are another detail that emphasizes and completes a traditional architectural look. Long before storm windows and heavy window glass were available, exterior shutters protected thin window panes and reduced drafts. To perform either of these functions, shutters had to completely cover the window. Therefore, to be authentic-looking, exterior shutters should be of a size that will do just that. However, interior shutters have also become a popular window treatment where control of

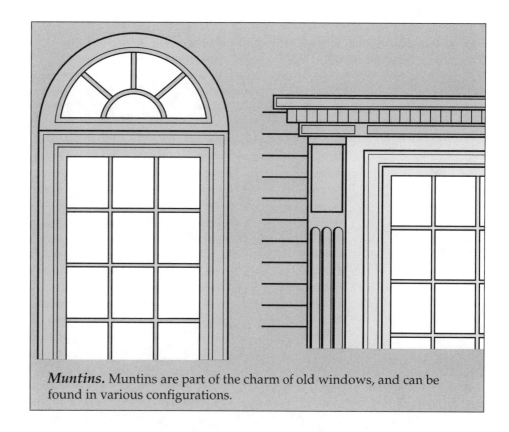

Muntins. Muntins are part of the charm of old windows, and can be found in various configurations.

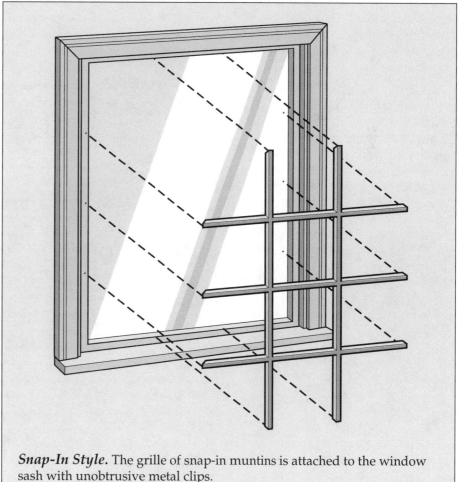

Snap-In Style. The grille of snap-in muntins is attached to the window sash with unobtrusive metal clips.

light, privacy, and ventilation are important or where the characteristic charm of shutters is desired.

Traditional exterior wood shutters are still sold, but shutters made of low-maintenance, weather-resistant, molded polystyrene also are available in wood-grain textures and a variety of basic colors. Operable shutters require good-quality, galvanized hinges that allow them to swing into position smoothly and be conveniently removed for cleaning.

Special Shutter Hardware. Shutters that you do not intend to open and close can be attached with screws, or hung on some special brackets that allow them to be removed easily for periodic maintenance.

Interior shutters are available pre-sanded and ready for painting or staining by the customer, and prestained that simply require wax or varnish. The louvers in shutters can be stationary or movable, horizontal, or vertical, and are available in patterns similar to those for exterior shutters.

To figure out how many shutters to buy, divide the width of the area to be covered by the number of panels desired (this should be an even number). For example, four panels in a 28-inch space will re-quire 7-inch panels. If fitting the shutters within the window opening, order either the

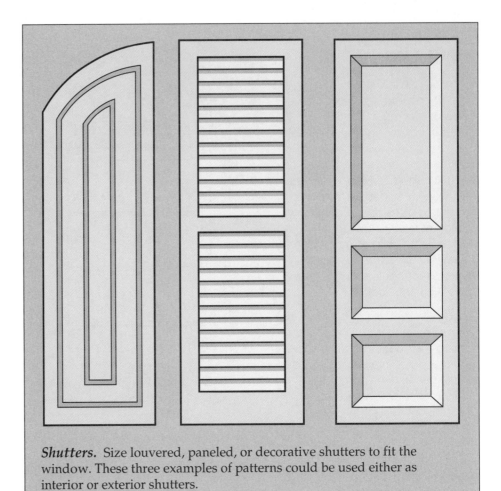

Shutters. Size louvered, paneled, or decorative shutters to fit the window. These three examples of patterns could be used either as interior or exterior shutters.

Fitting the Shutters

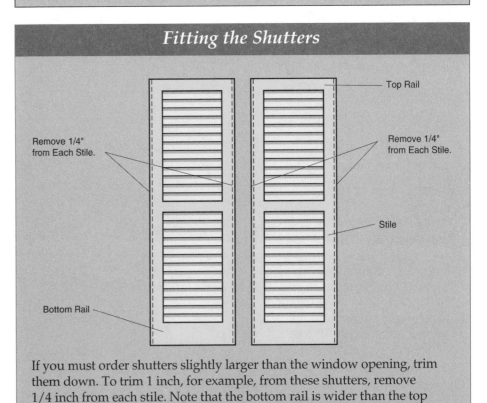

Top Rail

Remove 1/4" from Each Stile.

Remove 1/4" from Each Stile.

Stile

Bottom Rail

If you must order shutters slightly larger than the window opening, trim them down. To trim 1 inch, for example, from these shutters, remove 1/4 inch from each stile. Note that the bottom rail is wider than the top rail should you need to trim the height.

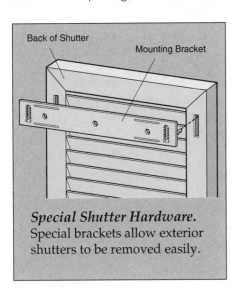

Back of Shutter

Mounting Bracket

Special Shutter Hardware. Special brackets allow exterior shutters to be removed easily.

exact size, or order the next larger size and trim each panel.

Let the dealer know if the shutters will be mounted inside or outside the window casing, so the dealer can recommend the correct hardware. When hanging shutters, rest each one on a coin. This will allow enough room to prevent the shutter from rubbing against the window sill once it's installed.

Interior Trim

"Trimming out" the window is the last step before painting it. The trim in this case refers to installing the stool, apron, and casing of the window (generally in that order). Many classic old houses feature ornately detailed window trim composed of many different shapes and sizes of wood. In fact, such trim sometimes served as the builder's signature, providing an occasion to showcase skills gained over many years. These days window trim is not quite so highly regarded, though it can still add a good measure of elegance and style to a room.

Trim is usually made from poplar, pine, Phillipine mahogany, or fir, though oak is sometimes used. When choosing wood at the lumber-yard, bear in mind that there may be several grades of material, some-times referred to by terms such as "stain grade" and "paint grade." Paint-grade material may have minor flaws (as well as differences in the grain or color of the wood) that will be concealed by a coat of paint. Increasingly, paint-grade material refers to wood that consists of numerous shorter lengths joined by interlocking finger joints and glue (paint will hide this fact as well). Stain grade material, on the other hand, is made from higher quality wood that will show no flaws when treated with a transparent or semi-transparent finish. To save money, don't buy stain-grade material if you are plan-ning to paint it. Trim is commonly available in lengths from 8 feet to 14 feet, in 2-foot increments.

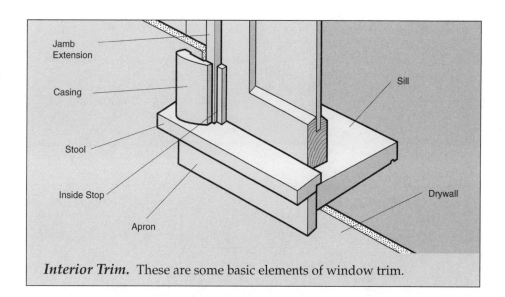

Interior Trim. These are some basic elements of window trim.

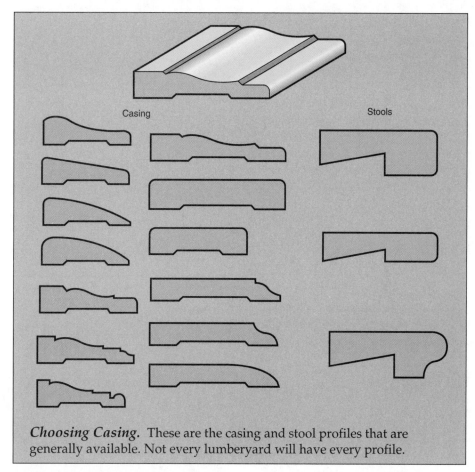

Choosing Casing. These are the casing and stool profiles that are generally available. Not every lumberyard will have every profile.

Choosing Casing. Casing comes in a great number of profiles. It ranges in width from 2 1/4 to 5 3/4 inches. Casing bridges the gap between the jamb and the wall covering, and provides a graceful finishing touch to the window. The stool provides a stop for the lower window sash, and extends the sill into the room. Part of the stool is angled to match the angle of the sill. The apron has a role similar to that of the casing, in that it covers the gap between the window jamb and the wall covering. The apron can be cut from the same material as the casing, or can be cut from different (and usually wider) stock.

Common Joinery for Trimwork

Wood trim can be installed in all sorts of ways to accentuate a particular decorative style, and may be anything from simple and understated to whimsical or even wildly imaginative. Nearly all installations, however, will use some version of two basic joints: the miter joint and the butt joint.

A miter joint occurs where two pieces of wood are joined together at an evenly divided angle. The angle most used in trim carpentry is 90 degrees, which means that each meeting trim piece must be cut to a 45-degree angle. A butt joint is the simplest joint of all; one of the meeting pieces is cut at a 90-degree angle and simply "butted" into an adjoining piece. Most window trim calls for combinations of miter joints and butt joints.

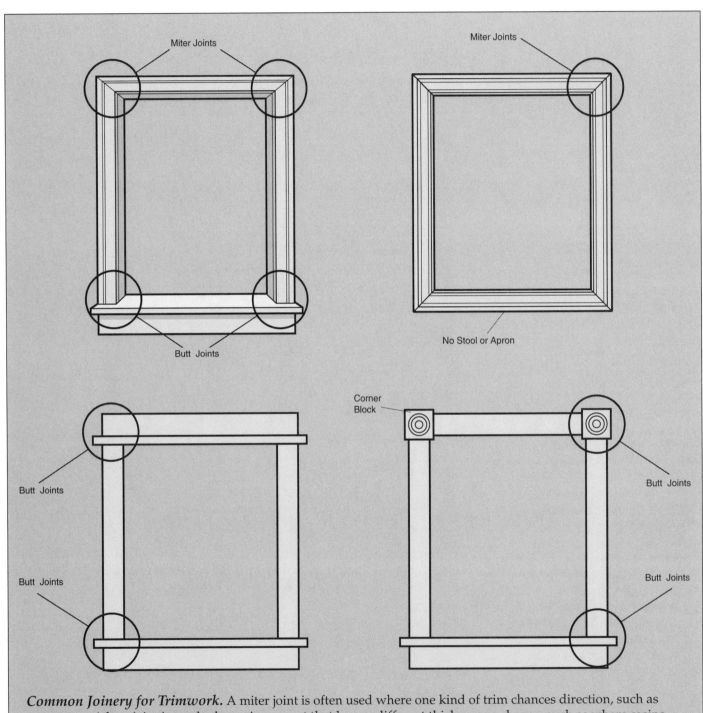

Common Joinery for Trimwork. A miter joint is often used where one kind of trim chances direction, such as at a corner. A butt joint is used where pieces meet that have a different thickness or shapes, such as where casing meets stool.

Installing the Stool

The stool should be installed before the casing and the apron. Some stools have an angled underside that matches the sill, while others are flat to match flat sills. In either case, installation is the same.

1 **Cutting the Stool.** First, cut the stool to length. Generally the "horn" of the stool extends slightly beyond the casing on both sides, but this is primarily an aesthetic decision so make it to your own tastes. Mark the center of the stool, and make a corresponding mark on the center of the window frame.

2 **Marking the Cut Lines.** Now hold the stool against the window jambs and align the two center marks. To lay out the horns, slide a combination square along the front edge of the stool until the blade rests against one side jamb of the window, and mark the stool as shown. Repeat this on the other side of the stool.

3 **Trimming the Stool.** While holding the stool against the casing, measure from its inside edge to the sash. Transfer this measurement to the marks just made in the previous step, then draw a perpendicular line from each point to the end of the stool. Cut the stool along the layout lines, using a hand saw or a saber saw. The stool should now fit into place on the window.

4 **Nailing the Stool.** Round over the edges of the stool and horn with sandpaper before installing it—don't forget to round the ends of the horns, too. Nail the stool into the window framing and set the nails.

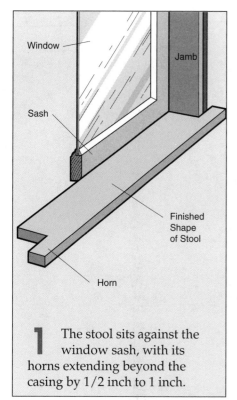

1 The stool sits against the window sash, with its horns extending beyond the casing by 1/2 inch to 1 inch.

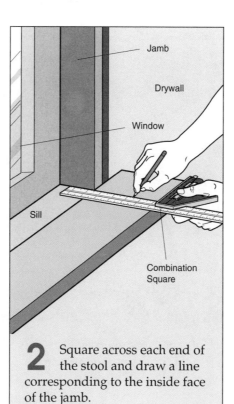

2 Square across each end of the stool and draw a line corresponding to the inside face of the jamb.

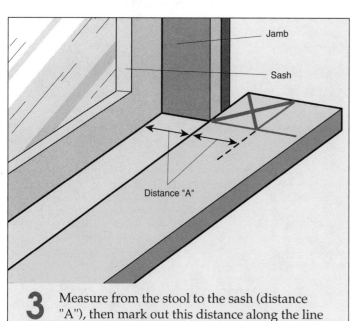

3 Measure from the stool to the sash (distance "A"), then mark out this distance along the line drawn in the previous step. Here the "X" marks the portion of stool that will be cut away.

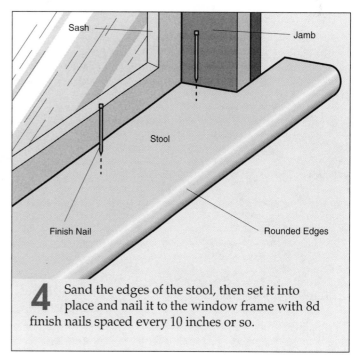

4 Sand the edges of the stool, then set it into place and nail it to the window frame with 8d finish nails spaced every 10 inches or so.

Installing the Apron

The apron is the simplest part of the window trim to install, but even here there's room for a bit of creativity. First, decide on how long to make the apron and on how to deal with its cut ends. Both decisions rest largely on personal taste. In terms of length, some people prefer the ends to line up with the outside of the casing, while others would rather they fall just short of the casing. The difference between the two amounts to fractions of an inch, but may have a significant visual impact.

The ends of the apron can simply be cut square and sanded smooth, or finished off with a flourish. Again, it is more of a personal preference. Experiment with a couple of different approaches to see which ones you like best.

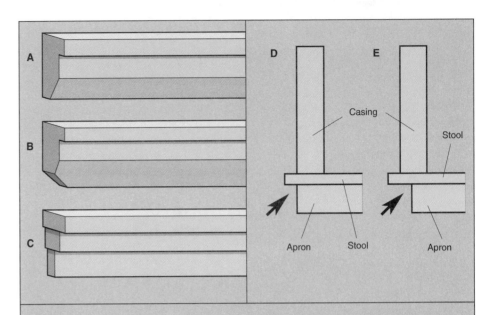

Installing the Apron. Ends cut square—(A) end grain shows, ends cut square, then lower corners cut at 45-degree angles—(B) end grain shows, (C) ends "returned"—no end grain shows. Generally the ends of the apron either (D) line up with the outside edge of the casing or (E) they stop short of that point.

Cutting a Returned Apron

Of the methods above, cutting a returned apron is most time consuming, but trim carpenters consider it the mark of a first quality job; many others just think it looks the best. This is because the profile on the face of the apron will turn the corner and "return" to meet the wall surface. No end grain is exposed; the ends of the apron are as smooth as its face. The drawings below show how to make a return. Note that these steps must be repeated for both ends of the apron.

1. Cut a 45-degree miter lengthwise through one end of the apron.

2. Cut a mating 45-degree miter in the end of a scrap piece of apron.

3. Place the scrap piece face down on the miter saw and cut off the very end just mitered. This will sever a small, triangular piece of the apron; set it aside for a moment.

4. Nail the apron in place beneath the window stool and glue the small "return" created in step "C" into place at the end of the apron. Secure the return with small brads, but do so cautiously to avoid splitting the return.

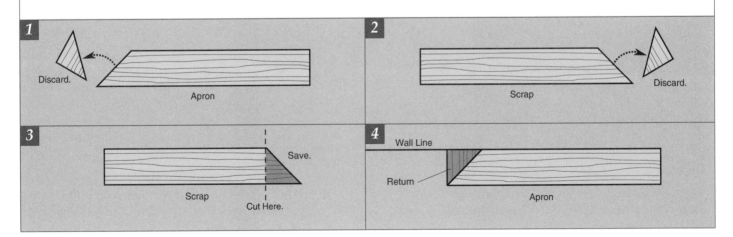

Casing a Window

With the stool and apron in place, it's time to case the window. Installing window casing is the fussiest part of trimming out a window—any imperfections in the joints will be readily apparent to anyone who cares to look. Making accurate joints may take some practice, but the process is really not difficult.

1 Marking the Reveals. The first step is to mark out reveals on the edges of the jambs. A reveal is a slight offset between the inside face of the jamb and the inside edge of the casing. It's easier to install the casings when not trying to make them perfectly flush with the inside face of the jamb, and they will look better, too. To mark the reveals, adjust the blade of a combination square to the size of the reveal and mark the jambs as shown.

2 Cutting the Side Casing. Each side casing will have a miter at one end and a square cut at the other. To find out how long the side casing should be, measure from the top of where head casing will rest down to the stool. Cut the bottom of one piece of side casing square. Place the piece along the side jamb reveal line. Mark where it intersects the head casing reveal line. Make the miter cut at this point. Repeat for the other piece of side casing. Tack the side casing in place. Leave the nail heads out, however, to reposition the casing, if necessary. When nailing the casing, line it up with the reveal marks.

3 Cutting the Head Casing. Miter one end of the head casing to meet the side casing. Miter the other end of the head casing to meet the other side casing.

4 Nailing the Casing. Fit the side casing into place, and trim it as necessary for a perfect fit. Cut and test the other side casing, and if all the joints look tight you can nail everything in place. Nail the casing into the jamb and into the studs behind the drywall.

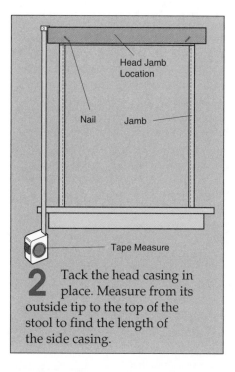

1 Mark the reveals along the edges of the window jambs. The reveal distance should be about 3/16 inch.

2 Tack the head casing in place. Measure from its outside tip to the top of the stool to find the length of the side casing.

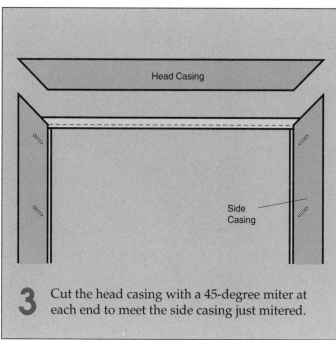

3 Cut the head casing with a 45-degree miter at each end to meet the side casing just mitered.

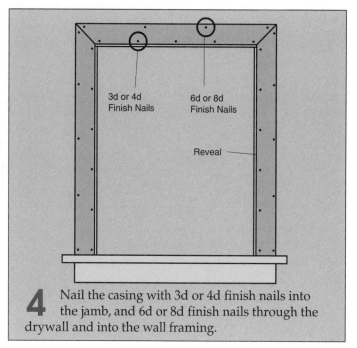

4 Nail the casing with 3d or 4d finish nails into the jamb, and 6d or 8d finish nails through the drywall and into the wall framing.

Window Repairs

Most window repairs are well within the capabilities of the do-it-yourselfer. When double-hung windows fail to operate properly, one of three problems probably exists. If the window won't budge, either it's been painted shut or one of the stop moldings has warped. If the window won't stay open or closed, the sash cord or spring balance must be adjusted or repaired.

Sash that have been painted shut can often be freed by slightly prying one of the stop moldings away from the window jamb. You may also have some luck simply pushing—firmly but not forcefully—against each stuck sash. The slight movement sometimes loosens up encrusted paint.

Replacing Cords in Double-Hung Windows

If the window won't stay open or closed, a sash cord is probably broken.

1. To gain access to a window's sash cord, the inside stop must be removed from both sides of the sash. And if the upper sash needs attention, the parting stops must come off, too. Carefully pry the stops away from the jambs with a wide putty knife.

2. Lift the sash clear of the stool and swing it out. With the sash free from the window, remove the sash cord from the keyed slot in its side. Then, remove the access panel, if the window has one. Inside the panel, the sash weight can be reached and removed. If there are no access panels, then the casing and wall material behind it will have to be removed to get at the weight.

3. Thread the new sash cord over the pulley and down into the sash weight cavity until it appears at the access panel. Tie the sash weight to the sash cord, then put the weight back into the cavity. Knot the other end of the sash cord at a point that will permit the weight to hang 3 inches above the sill when the sash is fully raised. Return the sash to its place and nail the stops to the jambs.

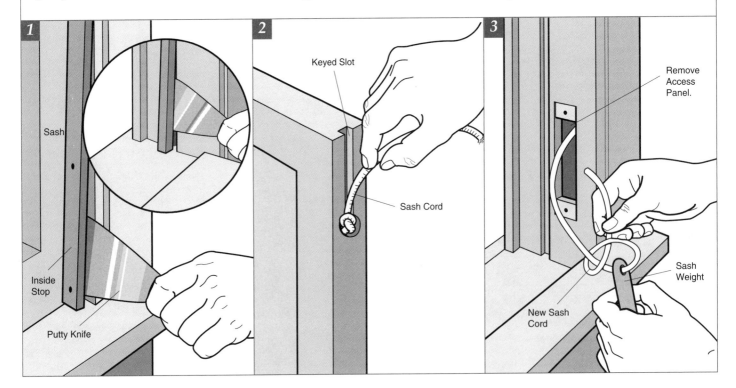

1. Sash / Inside Stop / Putty Knife

2. Keyed Slot / Sash Cord

3. Remove Access Panel. / Sash Weight / New Sash Cord

Replacing Balances

Occasionally, a spring or a spiral twist rod inside the balance tube breaks. When this happens, the entire assembly must be replaced.

1 **Removing the Screw.** Start by removing the screw holding the balance tube to the window jamb. Let the balance unwind fully, then remove the stops holding the window in place. (With some brands, the jambs are spring loaded, so just force the sash to one side and release it.)

2 **Removing the Sash.** With windows that do not have spring-loaded jambs, pry out the sash with a pry bar or other suitable tool, while being careful not to damage the surrounding woodwork.

3 **Replacing the Tube.** Once the sash is free, turn it onto its side and remove the screws holding the balance tube to the sash. Position the new assembl y in its channel, then fasten it to the sash as before. Reinstall the sash in the window, replace the stops if necessary, increase tension on the balance by rotating it clockwise several times, and fasten the tube to the jamb.

Adjusting Balances

Sometimes, when a window fitted with spring balances has remained closed for a long time, its springs weaken. If they have, the window won't stay open as it should.

1. Correct weak springs by adjusting the balances. First close the window, then remove the screw holding the balance tube to the jamb. Make sure to keep the tube from rotating counter-clockwise and losing still more tension.

2. Now rotate the tube three or four revolutions in a clockwise direction to tighten the spring inside the tube. Reposition the tube against the jamb and secure it by driving the screw into the jamb. Repeat this same procedure with the sash's other balance.

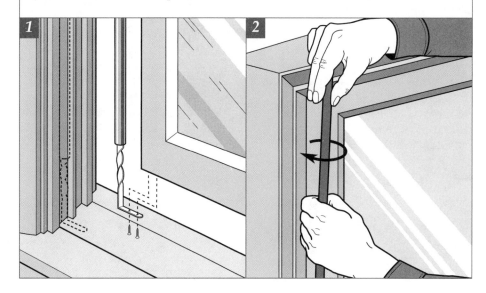

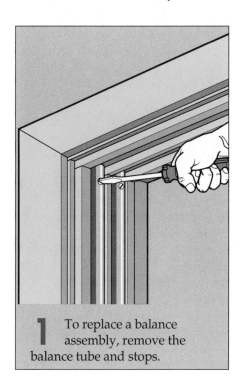

1 To replace a balance assembly, remove the balance tube and stops.

2 Pry out the sash in windows that do not have spring-loaded jambs.

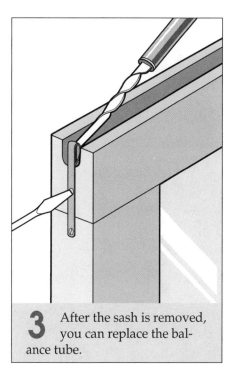

3 After the sash is removed, you can replace the balance tube.

Replacing Metal-Framed Screening

To replace a metal-framed screen, start by laying the screen on a worktable or other flat surface. Metal-framed screens are held in place by a vinyl spline that fits into a channel that runs the entire perimeter of the frame. To remove the spline, insert the tip of a flat-bladed screwdriver into the channel and pry up on it. Once the spline is started, the remainder pulls easily out of the channel.

1 **Cutting the Screening.** Separate the damaged screening from the frame. After squaring-up the frame, lay a piece of replacement screening over the frame. Using a pair of tin snips, cut a slightly oversized piece of material. (Generally, cutting it to the same dimensions as the frame's outside measurements works well.)

2 **Creasing the Screening.** Place the new screening over the opening in the frame and, using a putty knife, awl, or other suitable tool, crease the screening down into the channel along one side. This is the edge of the screening that will be stretched first.

3 **Inserting the Spline.** Now insert new spline using a hammer and wooden block or a screening tool. Then while someone pulls the screening taut, drive a second spline into the opposite channel. Start either of the two remaining sides of the screen as before and repeat the stretching process. Finish the project by trimming the excess screening.

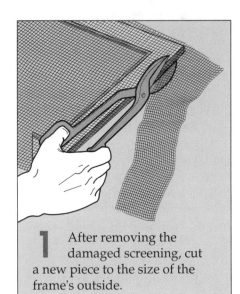

1 After removing the damaged screening, cut a new piece to the size of the frame's outside.

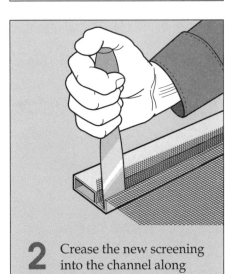

2 Crease the new screening into the channel along one side.

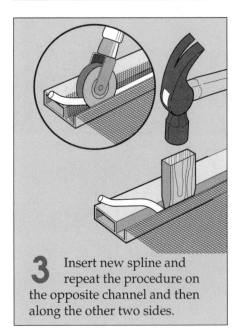

3 Insert new spline and repeat the procedure on the opposite channel and then along the other two sides.

Repairing & Replacing Screening

Damaged window screening can sometimes be repaired, but screens with major damage will probably have to be replaced.

■ If a screen has only a small tear, one quick, easy way to repair it—in either fiberglass or metal screening—is with clear silicone adhesive. Just dab it over the tear and let the glue set. Several coats may have to be applied to close the hole.

■ Metal screening also responds well to "darning" with strands of scrap screening. Unravel a strand or two and, using a sewing needle, weave the strands into the undamaged screen.

■ With larger holes, consider applying a patch. To make a repair of this type in metal screening, first square off the hole's edges with tin snips. Then cut a piece of scrap screening that's about 2 inches larger than the damaged area. Unravel a couple of the patch's strands on each side and bend them at a 90-degree angle. Fit the patch over the opening and insert the strands through the screening. When the patch is adequately positioned, bend the wires over to secure it.

■ A similar technique can be used to mend fiberglass screening. Again, square off the damaged area, cut an oversized patch from scrap material, and affix it with clear silicone glue.

Replacing Wood-Framed Screening

Though there are various methods for installing screen in wood frames, the following method is common and easily accomplished. The screening is held in place by staples that are driven all along the perimeter of the sash. A heavy-duty stapler and 1/4-inch staples are best for this job—do not use a household stapler.

To begin the job, remove the existing screening. Wood molding conceals the staples, so you'll have to remove it. Gently pry up each strip, using a putty knife. Be very careful because older molding can become quite brittle. Remove the staples holding the screening to the frame and discard the old screening.

1 **Cutting the Screening.** Unroll the replacement screening and cut a piece that is several inches wider and at least 12 inches longer than the frame. Fold over the top edge of the screening about 1/2 inch and staple this hemmed double layer to the sash, working out from the center to the edges.

2 **Stretching the Screening.** To ensure an adequate amount of tension on the screening, fashion a make-shift "stretcher" of a pair of 1x2s. Cut two 1x2s as long as the window is wide, then nail one of them to a piece of plywood laid on your workbench. Position the screen and sash with the excess screening overlapping the nailed-down 1x2. Nail a second 1x2 to the one already in place.

3 **Tightening the Screening.** Cut a length of 1x4 lumber lengthwise from corner to corner; this will yield two wedge-shaped pieces. With the wedges lying flat, insert them into the space between the 1x2s and the frame. Then tap the wedges with a hammer, alternating sides until the screening becomes taut.

4 **Attaching the Screening.** Staple the bottom edge of the

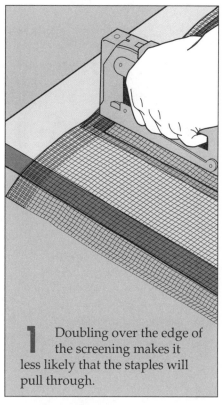

1 Doubling over the edge of the screening makes it less likely that the staples will pull through.

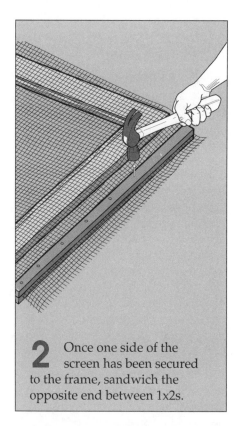

2 Once one side of the screen has been secured to the frame, sandwich the opposite end between 1x2s.

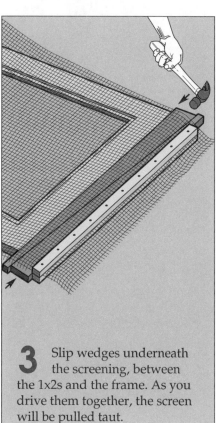

3 Slip wedges underneath the screening, between the 1x2s and the frame. As you drive them together, the screen will be pulled taut.

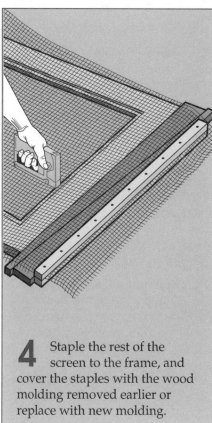

4 Staple the rest of the screen to the frame, and cover the staples with the wood molding removed earlier or replace with new molding.

screening in place, again working from the center outward to each edge. For the sides, pull the screen taut and staple from the center

outward, smoothing the mesh. Trim the excess screening from the frame with a utility knife and replace the molding.

Replacing Broken Glass

Not only do broken or cracked panes of glass allow the transfer of heat and moisture from one side of the window to the other, they are also a potential hazard. In older single-pane windows, homeowners can make the repairs by using replacement glass cut to the correct size, push-type glazier's points, and glazing compound. To figure the size of pane needed, measure the length and width of the opening and subtract 1/8 inch from each dimension. Standard replacement glass can be purchased at some hardware stores and all glass companies. Always wear gloves when handling glass.

The following steps explain the procedure for replacing glass in single-paned windows. If a newer, energy-efficient, double- or triple-paned window needs repair, contact a dealer for professional help.

1 Removing Glass. If possible, make the repair with the window in place because removing a window sash can be time consuming. Start by removing any glass shards, and chipping off any glazing compound with a putty knife. (Any compound that won't budge can be removed by heating it with a soldering iron.) To enable the new compound to adhere better, use a window scraper to rough up the base of the recess that the new glass will rest in.

2 Spreading the Glazing Compound in the Recess. Prepare the replacement pane of glass. To prepare the recess for the glazing compound, prime it with linseed oil, turpentine, or oil-based paint. If priming is not done, the untreated wood will draw oil from the glazing compound and poor adhesion will result. Prior to inserting the new glass, spread a 1/8-inch base of glazing compound along the base of the recess to create a seal and provide a cushion on

1 Remove glass shards and old glazing compound, but be very careful to wear heavy gloves and eye protection. (The glass may shatter and send flying shards toward your face.)

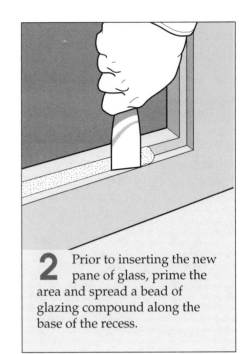

2 Prior to inserting the new pane of glass, prime the area and spread a bead of glazing compound along the base of the recess.

Glazier's Point

3 After inserting the glass, press glazier's points with putty knife around the edge of the glass—two or three per side.

4 Angle the compound with a putty knife in order that water will drain away from the glass.

which the glass rests. Now, carefully position the glass; be sure to apply enough, but not too much, pressure to the pane so the glazing compound spreads.

3 Inserting the Glazier's Points. Once the glass is firmly in place, secure it by pressing several glazier's points along each edge of the glass into the surrounding sash. Generally, a putty knife is the best tool for this operation. Be sure when doing this not to press hard against the glass.

4 Finishing the Installation. Shape some glazing compound into 1/4-inch-diameter rope. Press it into place along the edge of the glass, making sure it adheres to both the glass and the sash. Using a putty knife, bevel the compound to ensure drainage away from the glass. If the compound sticks to the knife, wet the blade with turpentine or linseed oil. Let the compound cure for a week before painting. Then allow the paint to overlap the glass by 1/16 inch to help seal the joint between the glass and the compound.

Reglazing Metal-Framed Windows

With metal-framed windows, the reglazing procedure depends on the construction of the frame. Many basement windows, for example, have a one-piece frame. With these, the glass is held in place with either spring clips and glazing compound or a vinyl spline.

Knock-Apart Frames. Other windows have knock-apart frames that can be disassembled in one of several ways.

■ To reglaze one-piece frame windows, chip away the glazing compound and remove the spring clips or pry out the spline with a screwdriver. Then, clean the channel in which the glass fits.

■ For windows with spring clips, lay a bead of compound along the flange the glass rests on, then position the glass, insert the clips, and fill the gap between the frame and glass with glazing compound. If the window has vinyl splines, position the glass and reinsert the spline, using the screwdriver.

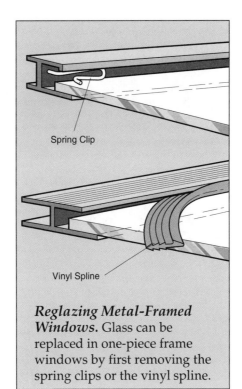

Reglazing Metal-Framed Windows. Glass can be replaced in one-piece frame windows by first removing the spring clips or the vinyl spline.

■ Repairing windows with knock-apart frames depends on the type. If the frames have screws, simply remove them, insert new glass, and reinsert the screws. If the frames have spring clips, pop them off, install new glass, and refit the clips.

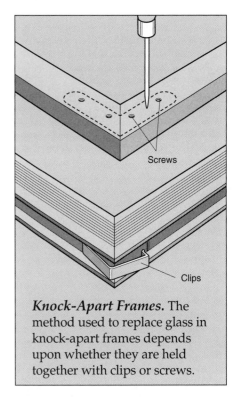

Knock-Apart Frames. The method used to replace glass in knock-apart frames depends upon whether they are held together with clips or screws.

■ If the windows have internal "L"-brackets in place at their corners, release them by drilling out the dimples. Make new dimples with an awl for the replaced brackets.

Cutting Glass

Always wear gloves whenever handling pieces of glass, and make sure that all children and animals stay out of the area. Be very careful when cutting glass because sharp edges are treacherous.

1. Using a measuring rule and framing square, determine the cutoff line. (Don't forget to make the pane 1/8 inch shorter and narrower than the size of the opening.) Then, using the framing square as a straightedge, score the glass with a glass cutter.

2. To fracture the glass, place a dowel beneath the score line. Press down firmly on each side of the line to snap the glass in two.

3. Glass usually snaps in a clean break. If not, the surface wasn't scored adequately. A jagged edge can be salvaged by nibbling off small pieces back to the score line using the notches on the glass cutter.

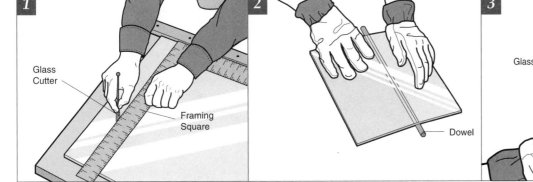

Weatherstripping Windows

The ever-increasing costs of energy have taught many homeowners that heat lost from the house through gaps around windows is like having a small hole in your pocket: you don't lose much each day, but over years the losses can be substantial. You don't have to replace all your old windows in order to save energy. In fact, one of the most cost-effective energy-saving tricks is also the easiest and least expensive: install weatherstripping.

Weatherstripping is only appropriate for windows that open. Fixed windows and skylights should be caulked and do not require weatherstripping. Always follow the specific installation instructions provided by the weatherstripping manufacturer.

There are two basic types of window weatherstripping. Compression-type consists of foam gaskets that can be applied to surfaces that close against each other. Some products are backed with self-adhesive strips to make installation easy. The drawback with compression-type weatherstripping is that the foam gaskets can't be used on surfaces that slide past each other, however.

For surfaces that slide past each other, spring-type weatherstripping is the best choice. It consists of flexible metal strips that close off gaps between parts of the window. Because they are metal, they wear well as the parts slide back and forth. Spring-type weatherstripping is typically secured to the window with brads, or sometimes with self-adhesive strips.

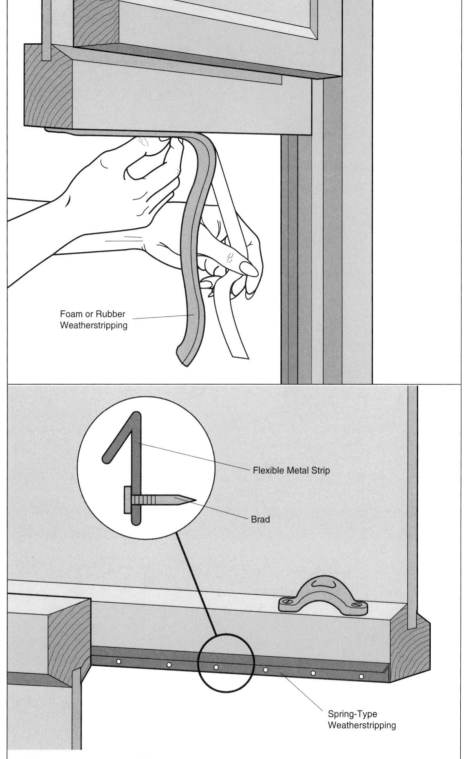

Foam or Rubber Weatherstripping

Flexible Metal Strip

Brad

Spring-Type Weatherstripping

Weatherstripping Windows. Foam weatherstripping is ideal for surfaces such as the window sash. Compressed against the sill when the window closes, it seals gaps and irregularities. The spring-type weatherstripping between the upper and lower sash of this window will prevent cold air from leaking in.

D O O R S

Doors are a buffer between the world outside and the privacy inside a home. But they can also add to the architectural style of a home and complement the decor of a room. Varying combinations of styles of doors, moldings, and door hardware can give a home a unique and personal look.

Various Door Styles

As you can see by paging through any manufacturer's catalog, doors are offered in dozens of shapes, sizes, colors, and materials. Most are made of wood, but you'll also find many doors made of metal, particularly those used as exterior doors.

Most wood doors are built in one of two ways: as individual panels set in a frame (called a panel door), or as a single plywood facing secured to each side of a lightweight wood framework (called a flush door). Either way, the composite assembly is very important because a door of solid wood alone would soon warp out of shape.

Panel Doors. Panel doors offer the widest variety of choices. They can be constructed with as few as three to as many as ten or more solid panels, in all sorts of shapes and size combinations. In fact, the panels do not even need to be made of wood. In some entry doors, for example, the bottom panels are wood while the top panels are glass.

Flush Doors. Flush doors come in a more limited range of variations, and are generally less expensive than panel doors because of their straightforward construction. You can enhance the simple lines of a flush door, however, by applying wood molding to its surface to give it a more traditional look.

Flush doors consist of a surface facing, sometimes called a skin, that covers either a solid or hollow core. Under the facing, the core can be hardwood, particleboard, cardboard, or even foam. The rails and stiles are concealed by the facing. The facing is usually made of thin plywood, but can also be vinyl- or metal-covered wood, aluminum, or even steel.

Metal Doors. Metal doors feature a core of rigid foam insulation surrounded by a metal skin. Often, the metal is embossed or stamped to give it the look of a wood door. These doors are very durable, and they don't warp as wood doors sometimes do. They are also very energy efficient. Installing a metal door is much like installing a wood door.

Sliding Doors. Patio, or sliding glass, doors consist of a large panel of glass framed with wood or metal. Usually, one side of the door is stationary while the other slides. Because these doors are exposed to the weather, the large expanses of glass should be double-glazed (two layers of glass separated by an airspace) to conserve energy. The frame may be wood, vinyl- or metal-covered wood, or aluminum.

Door Elements. Various configurations of the different door elements define a door's architectural character. The rails, for example, can be in the shape of a cross or an "X." Door hardware, too, is effective in defining style. Heavy hinges may be needed to support a heavy door, but they can be highly decorative, too. Similarly, door knobs, locks, and other decorative hardware can highlight the style of a door.

Interior doors express the style of a home and complement a chosen room decor. Interior doors can be customized with hardware and woodwork, although they are generally not as decorated or detailed as exterior doors. It is important to consider more than just cost when deciding on a style for your interior door. For example, a flush door used in a colonial style house, while cheaper than the more appropriate paneled door, will likely detract from the look of the house. Thus, the monetary savings is overshadowed by the loss of aesthetic harmony.

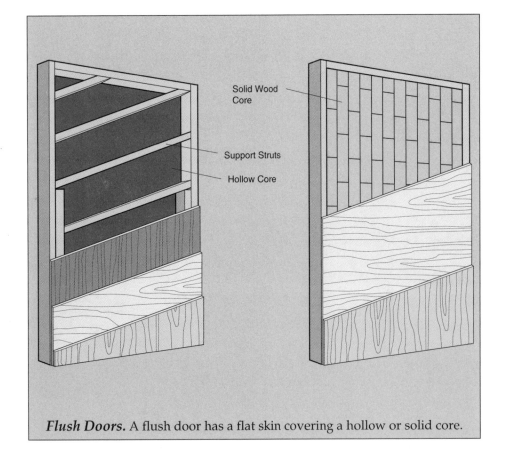

Solid Wood Core

Support Struts

Hollow Core

Flush Doors. A flush door has a flat skin covering a hollow or solid core.

Louvered Panel Door

Panel Door with Glazing

5-Panel Door

10-Panel Door

Dutch Door

Sliding Door

French Doors

Flush Door

Various Door Styles. Doors vary in appearance and construction, as well as in the way they open and close. Their designs vary to suit different functions and architectural styles.

Locating Elements within Walls

Many homes—especially older homes or homes that have had sections added on—are not laid out for the traffic flow of contemporary families and lifestyles. Installing a door where a solid wall had been often makes it much easier to get from one part of the house to another. But before you can install the door and the door jambs, you will have to create an opening in the wall that will maintain the structural integrity of your home.

First, decide on the location for the door, and check for any pipes, heating and cooling ducts, or electrical wires in the area. Wires can be rerouted fairly easily, but pipes and ducts are more difficult. If possible, change the location of the door to avoid any such obstructions. To find out what might be inside the wall, some detective work must be done. Secure the plans to the house, check the wiring, plumbing, and heating diagrams for clues to the whereabouts of these systems. Look directly above and below the wall—you may be able to learn something by checking in the attic or the basement. A magnet is very helpful in locating framing members—draw it back and forth across the wall to locate the heads of hidden nails holding wall coverings to the framing. When you finally begin to open up the wall, proceed carefully just in case there's a wire or pipe in there that you still don't know about.

Essential Parts of a Wood Door

All wood-panel doors consist of rails, stiles, panels, and mullions. The number and size give us different door styles.

■ Rails serve as the horizontal framing members at the top and bottom of the door; a center rail is part of many designs.

■ Stiles serve as the vertical framing members on each side of the door. The one on the lock side is the lock stile; the other is the hinge stile.

■ Panels are the areas framed by the rails. They may match the rest of the door, or they may be glass or some other material.

■ Mullions are the vertical members separating the panels.

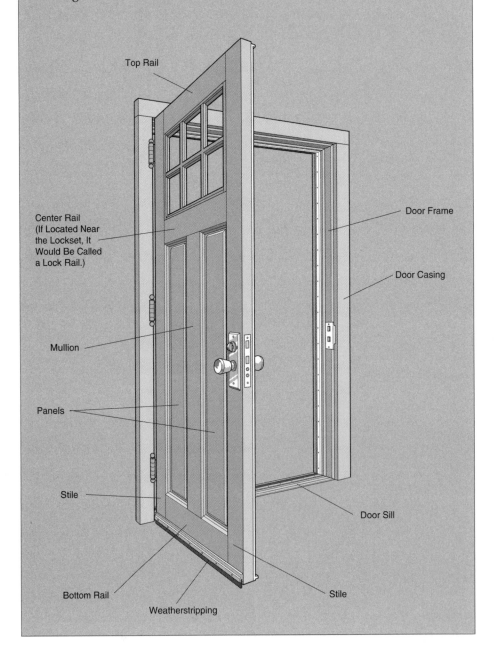

Top Rail

Center Rail (If Located Near the Lockset, It Would Be Called a Lock Rail.)

Door Frame

Door Casing

Mullion

Panels

Stile

Door Sill

Bottom Rail

Weatherstripping

Stile

Door Hardware

Some type of door hardware is needed for every door. Though the most important requirement for hardware is that it is functional, hardware can be ornamental as well. Hinges, locksets, escutcheon plates, and mail slots, for example, are all functional and highly decorative additions. When purchasing hardware, look for heavy-gauge metal, fine machining without sharp or rough edges, and a plated finish to withstand heavy use.

Match the hardware to the door. Not only must it blend with the style or type of door, but it must also do its job properly. A solid, heavy entry door, for instance, must be hung with heavy-duty hinges. Think about security as well when selecting hardware such as locksets and dead-bolt assemblies.

Door hardware is available in many styles, from sleek and contemporary to detailed European designs, and in various materials from burnished aluminum to solid brass.

Locksets. The term lockset refers collectively to the complete latch-bolt assembly, trim, and handles, knobs, or levers. A latch bolt is a spring-loaded mechanism that holds a door closed and may or may not have a lock incorporated in it. A dead bolt, on the other hand, is not spring loaded and can be operated only with a key or a thumbturn.

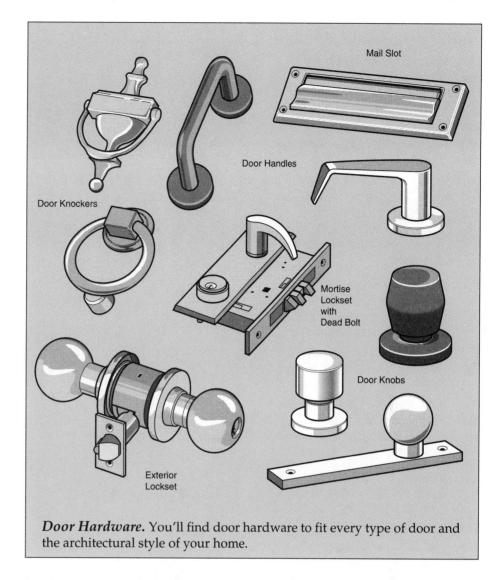

Mail Slot

Door Handles

Door Knockers

Mortise Lockset with Dead Bolt

Door Knobs

Exterior Lockset

Door Hardware. You'll find door hardware to fit every type of door and the architectural style of your home.

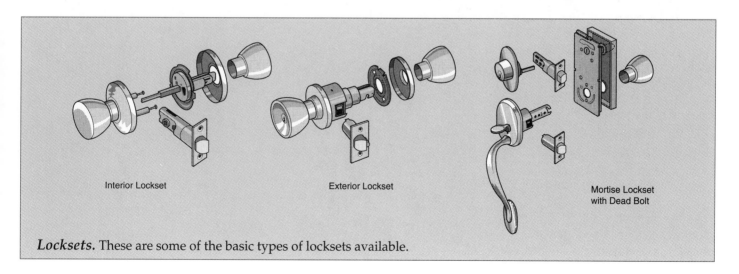

Interior Lockset

Exterior Lockset

Mortise Lockset with Dead Bolt

Locksets. These are some of the basic types of locksets available.

Installing a Lockset

The following steps explain the basic procedure for installing a lockset, although you should always refer to the instructions that come with most sets.

1 Locating the Holes. Using an awl and the template included with the instructions, mark positions for the knob assembly holes. The knob should be 37 inches from the floor. Its hole should be 2 3/8 inches or 2 3/4 inches from the edge of the door.

2 Drilling the Holes. Bore a hole into the door to the size specified for the lock tube. Next, drill a hole into the edge of the door for the latch and assembly. Drill first from one side, then from the other to avoid splintering the wood.

3 Installing the Lockset. Insert the cylinder assembly and latch into the door. Mortise the latch plate into the door.

4 Marking the Door Edge. Place the strike plate over the door latch, and mark the plate's position on the door edge.

5 Centering the Latch. With a sharp pencil, pinpoint the spot where the center of the latch hits the door jamb.

6 Marking Out the Strike Location. Hold the strike plate to the door jamb, centering the hole over the pencil mark made for the latch. Also, make sure it is flush with the top and bottom marks, indicating the edge of the door. Trace the location of the strike plate and the latch on the door jamb.

With a sharp wood chisel, cut a mortise into the jamb equal to the depth of the strike plate. If the cut is made too deep, use cardboard to raise the plate so it is flush. To make room for the latch, use a drill or chisel to bore a hole into the center of the strike plate. Fasten the strike plate to the jamb with screws, after checking the alignment again.

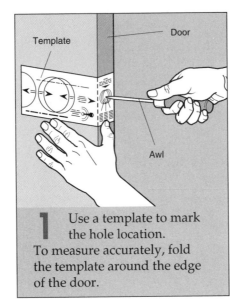

1 Use a template to mark the hole location. To measure accurately, fold the template around the edge of the door.

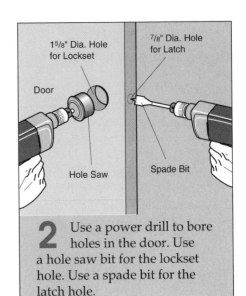

2 Use a power drill to bore holes in the door. Use a hole saw bit for the lockset hole. Use a spade bit for the latch hole.

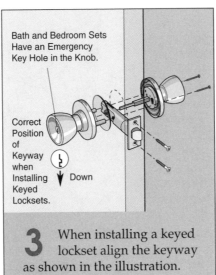

3 When installing a keyed lockset align the keyway as shown in the illustration.

4 Mark the position of the plate on the door edge. This will help when aligning the plate on the door jamb.

5 Remove the plate and close the door. Find the location of the strike.

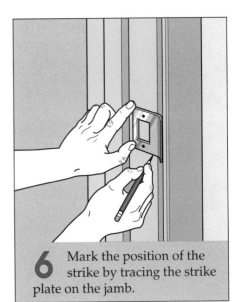

6 Mark the position of the strike by tracing the strike plate on the jamb.

Customizing Doors

An attractive door is just the beginning of a welcoming entry. Details and accessories that are designed to highlight doors include decorative hardware, lintels, pediments, sidelights, fanlights, transoms, and a variety of molding.

Exterior Details

Outside detail work requires a good coat of exterior trim paint after installation. Except for window-paned details, such as sidelights, which should be installed with the door, most details can be added after the rest of the door is in place.

■ Sidelights, or narrow windows flanking a door; fanlights, or semicircular ribbed windows usually placed over a door; and transoms or horizontal windows placed directly above a door, add natural light to a heavily used, but often dimly lit, area. All three must be allowed for when laying out the rough door opening.

■ Pediments, or millwork that sets above doors, originated in Greece.

A pediment is solely decorative and is added either after a new door is installed or to a pre-existing door.

■ Pilasters, or columnlike adornments used to flank an entry, are also purely decorative and can be added at any time.

■ Lintels are horizontal members that span the door opening. Structural lintels support the weight of the wall above; decorative lintels simply help to unify the various visual elements of the door surround.

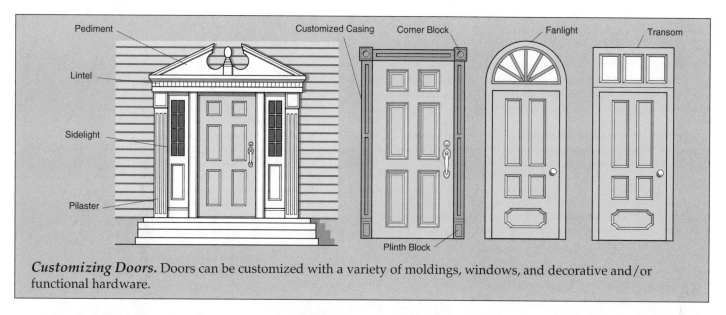

Customizing Doors. Doors can be customized with a variety of moldings, windows, and decorative and/or functional hardware.

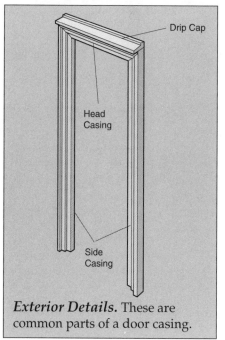

Exterior Details. These are common parts of a door casing.

Interior Details

Casing can be simple or complex, depending on the wood, joinery, and detailing. Door trim is easy to recognize, and it can be manipulated in dozens of ways.

■ Head casing is the horizontal member that spans the top of the door frame.

■ Side casing consists of the trim on either side of the door. Like the head casing, side casing is nailed into the edge of the door frame.

■ Corner blocks are decorative blocks that can be used to make the transition between horizontal members and vertical members.

■ Plinth blocks are used at the bottom of the side casing where baseboard meets the door trim.

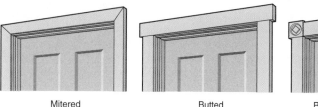

Mitered   Butted   Butted to Corner Blocks

Installing Mitered Door Trim

There are several ways to join head casing to side casing around a door. The most common method is to use a miter joint, which is simply two 45-degree angles joined to make a 90-degree angle. You can use other joints, however, depending on your skill and the architectural style of your house.

1 **Marking the Reveal.** The inside edge of the casing should be offset from the inside edge of the jambs by approximately 3/16 inch. The small edge caused by offsetting the two is called a reveal. Set the combination square for 3/16 inch and use it to guide your pencil around the jamb, leaving a line 3/16 inch from the edge.

2 **Making the First Miter.** Cut a length of casing square at one end. Then place the casing against the reveal line, and square cut against the floor. Mark the casing at the point where the vertical and horizontal reveal lines intersect, and cut a 45-degree angle at this point.

3 **Making the Next Miters.** Nail the first piece of casing to the jamb with 3d or 4d casing nails spaced every 12 inches or so. Now cut a 45-degree angle on another piece of casing, fit it against the side casing, mark it for the opposite 45-degree angle, then cut and install it.

4 **Completing the Final Miters.** After installing the head casing, mark, cut, and install the final length of side casing.

5 **Setting the Nails.** After nailing the casing in place, set all the nails just below the surface of the wood, then fill the holes with wood putty and sand them smooth when dry. Use a nail set and a lightweight hammer to set the nails. In a pinch, though, carefully use a 10d nail as a makeshift nail set.

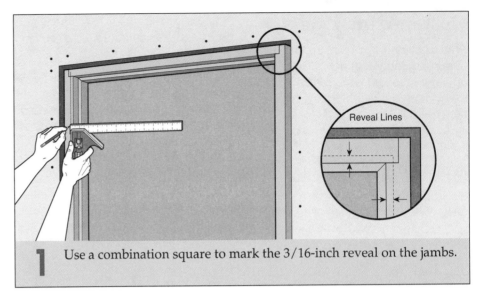

1 Use a combination square to mark the 3/16-inch reveal on the jambs.

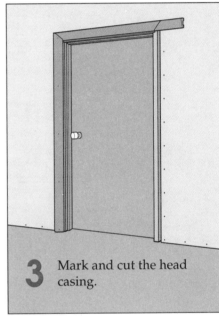

Reveal Lines

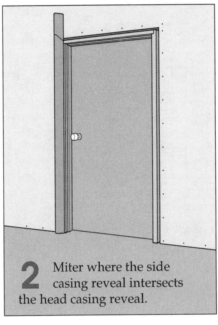

2 Miter where the side casing reveal intersects the head casing reveal.

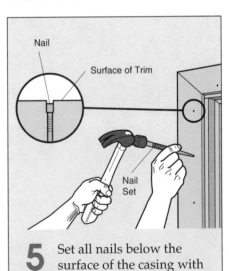

3 Mark and cut the head casing.

4 Mark and cut the second side casing.

Nail
Surface of Trim
Nail Set

5 Set all nails below the surface of the casing with a nail set and a hammer.

All residential doors hang in a wood frame made of these elements.

■ The head jamb is at the top, flanked by side jambs, one on the lock side and one on the hinge.

■ The sill, or threshold, which is often eliminated on interior doors, lies underfoot.

■ Stops, narrow strips of wood nailed to the head and side jambs, prevent the door from swinging too far when it closes.

■ The strike plate, or the metal strip mortised into the side jamb on the lock side of the door, accepts the latch.

■ Wood casings at the top and sides cover the framework, any gaps, and add the finishing touch to the installation.

■ Weatherstripping, ideally incorporating interlocking metal strips, should be included all around the frame of an exterior door.

■ The door frame is nailed within a "rough opening" in the wall formed by wall studs and a header (the framing of interior walls does not always require a header, however.) The rough opening is always large enough so that the door frame can be slipped into place and adjusted vertically or horizontally. Pairs of wood shims are slipped between the door frame and the studs to adjust the door frame and are cut flush with the door frame later on.

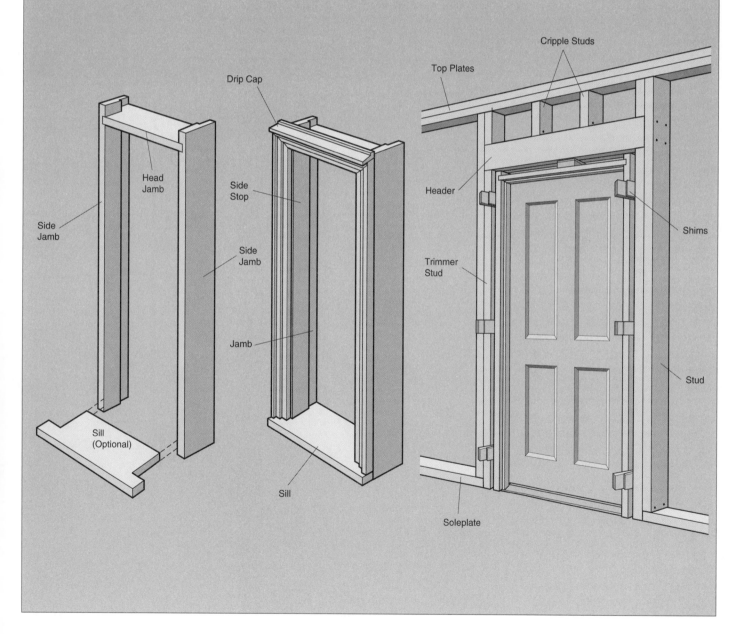

Building a Frame & Hanging a Door

Making a frame and hanging a door within it takes more time than installing a prehung door, but it usually costs less. In addition, it allows you to fit the frame to walls of non-standard thickness.

1 Assembling the Jambs.
Purchase nominal 1-inch jamb stock at the lumberyard or home center. The most commonly available jamb stock is 4 1/2 inches wide to equal the thickness of a 2x4 wall with 1/2-inch drywall on each side. You can also buy adjustable split jambs for walls of non-standard thickness. (See page 55.) The side jambs will come with dadoes to accept the head jamb. Allowing for the depth of the dadoes, cut the head jamb to length so that the opening will be 1/4-inch wider than the door. Cut the side jambs to length so that the distance from the top jamb to the floor equals the length of the door plus 1/2-inch. This will give the door 1/8-inch clearance at top and side and 3/8 inch clearance at the bottom. Nail the side jambs to the head jamb with three 8d nails on each side, and set the frame into the rough opening.

2 Plumbing the Jambs. Level the head jamb as needed by shimming up the bottoms of the side jambs. Then you should plumb one of the side jambs with a 4-foot level, using a pair of shims to adjust the jamb in or out as needed. If you don't have a 4-foot level, use a standard level and hold it against a long, straight board instead. Nail through the jamb and into the first pair of shims with one 8d casing nail.

3 Shimming the Jambs. Continue to plumb, shim, and nail the first jamb. Use three or four pairs of shims: near the head, in the middle, and near the bottom of the door frame. Now plumb the other jamb, making sure it is the same distance from the first jamb along its entire

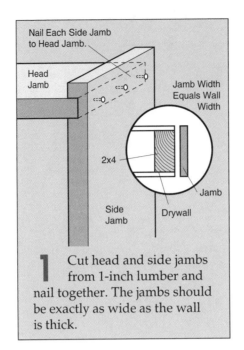

1 Cut head and side jambs from 1-inch lumber and nail together. The jambs should be exactly as wide as the wall is thick.

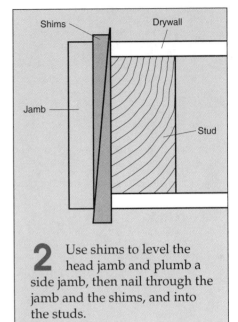

2 Use shims to level the head jamb and plumb a side jamb, then nail through the jamb and the shims, and into the studs.

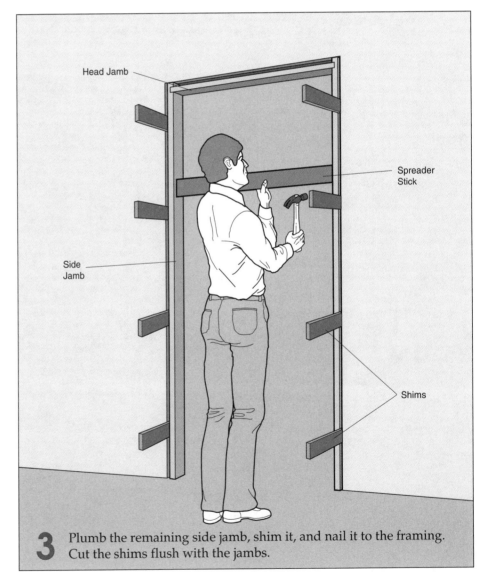

3 Plumb the remaining side jamb, shim it, and nail it to the framing. Cut the shims flush with the jambs.

length. To keep from having to measure this distance repeatedly, cut a scrap piece of wood to the exact distance required between the jambs, and use this "spreader stick" to gauge the opening for placing the shims.

4 Fitting the Door. If you must trim the top or bottom of a hollow core door, never remove more than 3/4 inch; more will weaken the structure of the door. Use a plane to bevel the knob side of the new door about 3 1/2 degrees; this will help it to close easier.

5 Installing Hinges. The size and number of hinges will vary, depending on the type and thickness of the door. Hollow-core doors, for example, are light and do not require as heavy a hinge as solid doors. Most doors should have at least three hinges, although hollow-core interior doors often have only two. The top hinge should be 7 inches from the top of the door, and the lowest hinge should be 11 inches from the bottom. Center the other hinges. Use a 1 1/4-inch wood chisel to mortise hinges level with the surface of the door edge, then screw each hinge to the door.

6 Installing the Door Stop. Temporarily tack the door stops to the jambs. They should be located so that the hinge side of the door is flush with the jambs.

7 Cutting Jamb Mortises. Now set the door into the jamb, using shims to position it squarely within the opening. Mark the top and bottom of all hinge leaves where they meet the door jamb. Remove the door and use a chisel to mortise the hinge locations on the jamb. (Many installers prefer to cut hinge mortises before installing the door frame in the rough opening.)

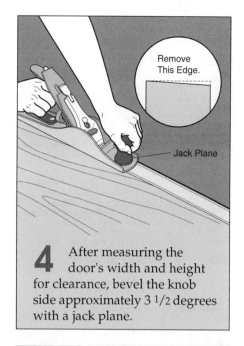

Remove This Edge.

Jack Plane

4 After measuring the door's width and height for clearance, bevel the knob side approximately 3 1/2 degrees with a jack plane.

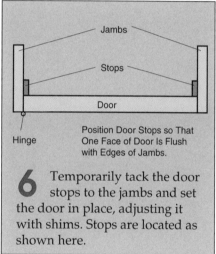

Jambs

Stops

Door

Hinge

Position Door Stops so That One Face of Door Is Flush with Edges of Jambs.

6 Temporarily tack the door stops to the jambs and set the door in place, adjusting it with shims. Stops are located as shown here.

8 Completing the Door. Remove the hinge pins, screw the loose hinge leaves to the door jamb, then place the door back into the opening and mate the hinge leaves by inserting the pins. Make sure the door swings freely. If it doesn't, adjust the hinges or door stops, or trim the door. Complete the door with molding and hardware. When hanging an exterior door, add weatherstripping. Paint or finish any door, particularly one leading outdoors, as soon as possible.

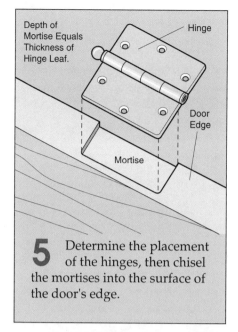

Depth of Mortise Equals Thickness of Hinge Leaf.

Hinge

Door Edge

Mortise

5 Determine the placement of the hinges, then chisel the mortises into the surface of the door's edge.

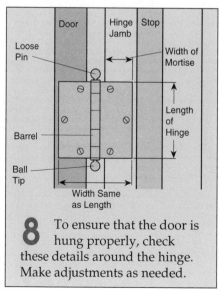

7 Mark the top and bottom of the hinge where it meets the side jamb. Loose pin hinges should be installed with the pin at the top.

Door

Hinge Jamb

Stop

Loose Pin

Width of Mortise

Length of Hinge

Barrel

Ball Tip

Width Same as Length

8 To ensure that the door is hung properly, check these details around the hinge. Make adjustments as needed.

Installing an Interior Prehung Door

1 Marking the Door Location. Use a level and a pencil to mark out the dimensions of the rough opening on one side of the wall. The width of the rough opening is the width of the door plus 2 1/2 inches; the height of the rough opening is the height of the door plus 3 inches.

2 Cutting the Opening. Remove the baseboard, and use a keyhole saw to cut through drywall or plaster along the layout lines. Be very careful not to cut through any wires or pipes. Remove the wall covering carefully to expose the interior of the wall. Removing plaster or drywall is very dusty business, so cover adjacent floors and move furniture well away. Remove studs from the opening by twisting them from the soleplate. Refer to the chart on page 55 to determine the proper dimension of header lumber to use. Cut off the studs that will become cripple studs. Leave the cripples long enough so that the properly sized header will be at the proper rough opening height.

3 Making the Header. Nail the two pieces of header lumber together with 16d nails, using a piece of 1/2-inch plywood to fit between the pieces as a spacer. Leave the short pieces in place to be attached to the header later. Use the chart on page 55 to determine the proper dimension of header lumber to use. Nail the two pieces of header lumber together with 16d nails, using a piece of 1/2-inch plywood cut to fit between the pieces as a spacer.

4 Installing the Header. Toenail the header in place—you can use scrap 2x4 stock to brace it carefully in place while you nail it.

5 Framing the Opening. To form the rough opening width, nail two 2x4s together and insert them between the header and soleplate at the rough opening width. Plumb, then nail them in place.

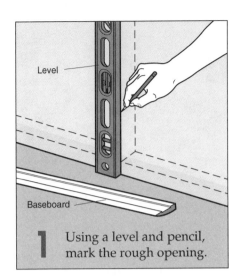

1 Using a level and pencil, mark the rough opening.

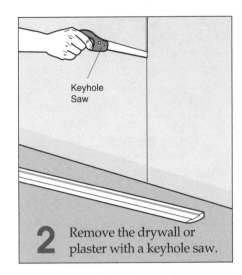

2 Remove the drywall or plaster with a keyhole saw.

3 Make the header of two pieces of framing lumber with 1/2-inch plywood between.

4 Toenail the header into place.

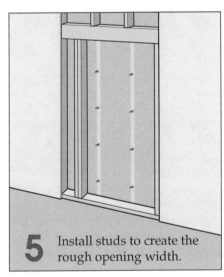

5 Install studs to create the rough opening width.

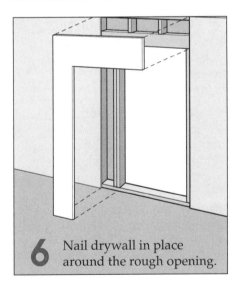

6 Nail drywall in place around the rough opening.

6 Complete the Opening. Use a keyhole saw to cut through he other side of the drywall, using the framing you just installed as a guide. Cut, fit, and nail drywall in place around the rough opening. With a handsaw and wood chisel, remove the section of the soleplate inside the rough opening. The framing is now ready to receive the prehung door unit.

Installing a Door with a Split Jamb

Before buying a prehung door (or preassembled unit), measure the jambs carefully to make sure they match the thickness of the wall where the door will be installed. Some prehung units have an adjustable jamb, called a split jamb. This kind of unit can easily be adjusted to fit walls of various thicknesses.

1 Preparing the Door Unit.
Remove the unit's packaging, which may include a wood spreader that secures the bottom ends of the side jambs. Separate both halves of the unit. Pull out the double-headed nail that holds the door to the jamb on the latch side, but do not remove any of the spacer blocks. Set the door and one half of the frame into the rough opening. Plumb the door frame, then nail the casing to the wall studs with 6d casing nails.

2 Installing the Second Half.
Move to the other side of the opening and slip wood shims between the jamb and wall framing at the point where the spacer blocks touch the door. Insert the second half of the frame into the mating groove of the first section and nail the casing to the wall. Then nail through the stop, jambs, and shims to secure the door. Open the door and remove the spacers. Check to see if the door works properly.

1 Secure the first half of a split-jamb door by nailing through the casing and into the wall.

Detail B

Detail A

2 Insert the second half of the door from the other side. Detail A fits the groove of detail B. Nail it in place through the side jambs.

Header Specs				
Span of Opening (in feet)				
4	**6**	**8**	**10**	**12**
Two 2x4	Two 2x6	Two 2x8	Two 2x10	Two 2x12
Two 2x6	Two 2x8	Two 2x10	Two 2x12	—
Two 2x10	Two 2x10	Two 2x12	—	—

Roof only
One-story
Two-story

Installing Bypass Doors

These lightweight wooden interior doors hang from rollers that slide in a track attached to the head jamb.

1 Installing the Guide Track. Once the door frame is in place, screw the guide track to the underside of the head jamb as per the manufacturer's directions.

2 Installing the Door Guide. Install the door guide in the floor, midway between both side jambs and directly below the guide track. You can use a plumb bob to find the proper location on the floor.

3 Installing the Doors. Lift one door into place and hook its rollers into the back portion of the track. Then lower the door into place in the guide track and slide it to one side of the opening. Repeat the procedure with the other door.

Tightening Loose Hinges

If the screws are loose, sometimes they can simply be tightened. However, if the screws cannot be tightened enough, replace them with larger diameter screws if the holes in the hinge leaves will accept them. If not, drill out the existing holes, insert 1/4-inch glue-coated wooden dowels, drill pilot holes, and drive the screws into the dowels.

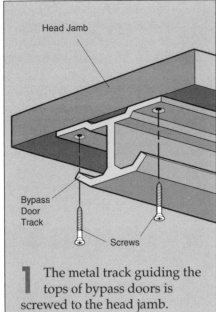

1 The metal track guiding the tops of bypass doors is screwed to the head jamb.

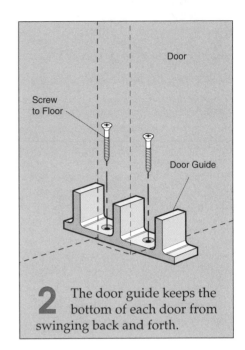

2 The door guide keeps the bottom of each door from swinging back and forth.

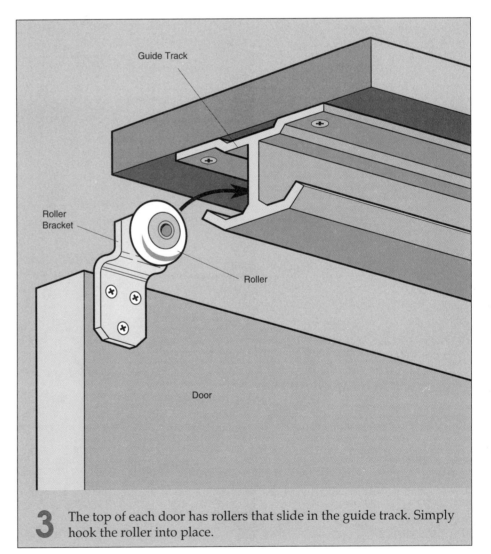

3 The top of each door has rollers that slide in the guide track. Simply hook the roller into place.

Aligning Double Doors

A set of double doors consists of two doors within a single door frame; a wood divider separates the doors from each other. In some cases there is a lockset on both doors, while in other cases only one of the doors has a lockset (the other may have lock bolts that slide into holes cut into the sill and the head jamb). Double doors are installed much like single doors, though their size makes them rather unwieldy—you'll need some help to maneuver the unit into place. Once the doors are installed, they must be aligned with each other.

1 Installing the Doors. Center, shim, and plumb the doors; treat the jamb for the bolted door similar to the hinge-side jamb of a single door. Loosen the pairs of shims behind the top and bottom hinges of both doors, then check the gap between the doors and the head jamb where the doors meet. Tighten the shims behind the top hinge of the higher door until the gap is equal for both doors; then tighten all of the shims, recheck the gap, and nail through the jamb of the inactive door with 16d galvanized finishing nails.

2 Adjusting the Jambs. Adjust the active-door jamb like the lock-side jamb of a single door, forcing it out with shims until the two doors line up perfectly. Adjust the gap between the side jambs and the doors like a single door.

3 Shimming the Head Jamb. Insert three sets of shims between the header and the head jamb and adjust them until the gap between the head jamb and the door is even, then drive two 16d finishing nails up through each set of shims into the header.

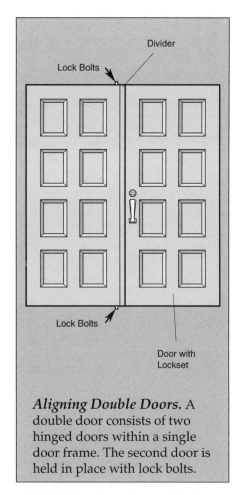

Aligning Double Doors. A double door consists of two hinged doors within a single door frame. The second door is held in place with lock bolts.

1 Shim carefully behind the hinges of double doors. Extra long screws used to attach hinges will hold the shims in place.

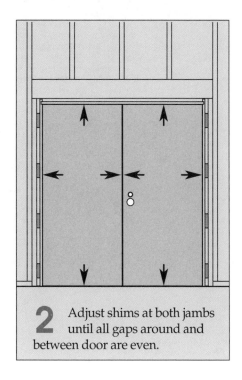

2 Adjust shims at both jambs until all gaps around and between door are even.

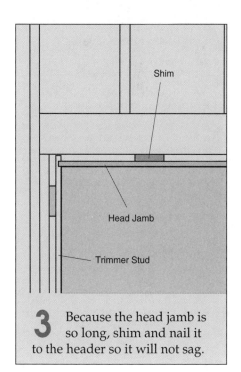

3 Because the head jamb is so long, shim and nail it to the header so it will not sag.

Installing Bifold Doors

A bifold door is commonly used on closets, particularly in bedrooms, because it folds neatly out of the way. Each door consists of two panels connected with leaf hinges. Mounting hardware at the top of each door fits into a guide track screwed to the head jamb, while hardware at the bottom fits into a small pivot bracket that is screwed to the floor.

1 **Installing the Guide Track.** First screw the upper guide track to the head jamb following manufacturer's instructions. To shorten the track to fit the opening, cut it with a hacksaw.

2 **Installing the Pivot Bracket.** Screw the pivot bracket to one of the side jambs; sometimes there will also be provision for running a screw into the floor.

3 **Installing the Door.** Install the rest of the mounting hardware on the doors; holes for these are usually predrilled by the manufacturer. Then tip the door into place, making sure the pivots at the top and bottom fit into their respective brackets. Tighten the top bracket to secure the door.

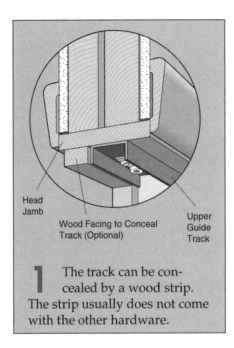

Head Jamb

Wood Facing to Conceal Track (Optional)

Upper Guide Track

1 The track can be concealed by a wood strip. The strip usually does not come with the other hardware.

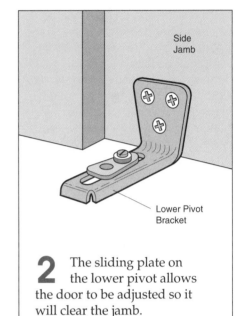

Side Jamb

Lower Pivot Bracket

2 The sliding plate on the lower pivot allows the door to be adjusted so it will clear the jamb.

Eliminating Squeaks

Pry up the hinge pins, then squirt some lubricating oil into the barrel. Open and close the door several times to allow the oil to work its way down. If that does not work, open the door fully, drive a shim under the hinge side of the door, and remove the hinge pins one at a time. Clean the barrel with a small wire brush. While each hinge pin is out, inspect it for rust buildup. Rusted pins can be polished with a grinder or a rust-removing solution. Even pins that are not rusted should be coated lightly with oil.

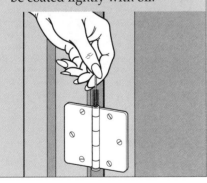

3 Set the lower pivot into the bracket and tip the door into place. Once the door is in place, tighten the fitting on the guide track to hold it in place.

Installing Swinging Passageway Doors

A full-sized swinging door is ideal between kitchens and dining areas. It can be pushed open from either direction and swings shut when released due to the action of a spring-operated bottom hinge. These hinges are secured to both the floor and the door's bottom edge.

1 Rounding the Edges. Using a jack plane or a router, round over the edges on both sides of the door.

2 Laying Out the Hinges. On the head jamb, mark the top-pivot location at the distance from the hinge-side jamb specified by the hinge manufacturer. Use a combination square to extend the mark across the width of the head jamb, and suspend a plumb line from the center of this line. Now measurethe distance between the side jamband the plumb line at several points. If the distance is

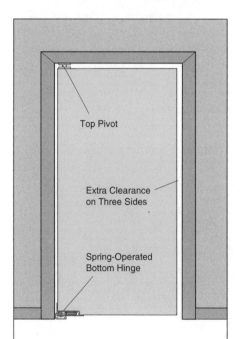

Installing Swinging Pas-sageway Doors. A full-length swing door rests between a bottom hinge and a top pivot. The door needs extra clearance to swing between the jambs.

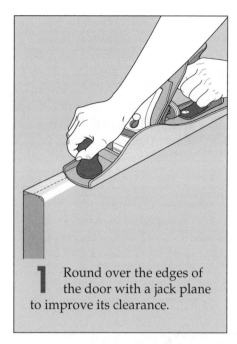

1 Round over the edges of the door with a jack plane to improve its clearance.

less than the door clearance given by the manufacturer, adjust the location of the top pivot accordingly. Mark the point where the plumb bob touches the floor.

2 Locate the bottom hinge by dropping a plumb bob and line down from the top pivot location.

3 Aligning the Pivot Plate. Measure the distance from the center of the pivot to one end and one side of the pivot plate. Mark the floor the same distances from

Choosing Door Hinges

Hinges vary greatly—from decorative to invisible, one-directional to two, self-closing to standards—in both appearance and function.

Most interior doors have common butt hinges, which are either right or left handed. A right-handed hinge is on the right when the door opens away from the person, and the opposite is the left-handed type. In either case, never try to use a hinge turned upside down because the pin will fall out.

The proper size and weight of a hinge depends on the thickness

and weight of the door. An average hollow-core interior door, for example, should have 3 1/2-inch, medium weight hinges.

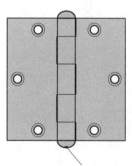

To Remove Hinge Pin, Insert Nail Here and Tap Upward with Hammer.

Door Hinge Sizes

Door Thickness	Door Width	Hinge Size
7/8" - 1 1/8" (screen or storm)	36" or less	3"
1 3/8" (passage)	32" or less	3 1/2"
	Over 32"	4"
1 3/4" (passage or entry)	36" or less	4 1/2"
	Over 36"	5"
2" (entry)	42" or less	5"–6"

the plumb-bob mark; align the pivot plate with these marks, centering it over the plumb-bob mark, and outline the plate on the floor.

4 **Installing the Top Pivot.** Drill a hole in the head jamb at the location of the top pivot to accommodate the top-pivot cap, then insert the cap in the hole. Mortise a recess for the wings of the cap, similar to mortising the leaf of a standard hinge as described on page 53. Turn the cap over and screw it to the jamb. To locate the pivot socket in the top of the door, subtract the clearance between the door and the side jamb (as specified by the pivot-hinge manufacturer)

from the top-pivot measurement on the head jamb. Mark the location on a centerline drawn along the top of the door, and drill and mortise for the pivot socket. Then screw the socket to the door.

5 **Mounting the Floor Hinge.** Starting at the bottom of the door, you draw a line on the face of the door 1/2 inch from the hinge-side edge. Align the floor-hinge assembly with the line and the bottom of the door. Outline the entire hinge with a pencil. At the top of the hinge, run a line across the edge of the door. Use a handsaw and a chisel to cut out all the wood within the outline, set the hinge in the cutout,

and fasten the hinge to the bottom of the door with wood screws.

6 **Completing the Installation.** Lift the door and fit the pivot socket over the pivot cap. At the bottom of the door, screw the pivot plate to the floor over the outline made for it in step 2. Center the door between the jambs by turning the alignment screw in the bottom hinge, and set the speed and force of the door's swing by adjusting the spring-tension nut. Finally, cover the hinge and the gap at the bottom corner of the door with the trim plates that have been provided by the manufacturer.

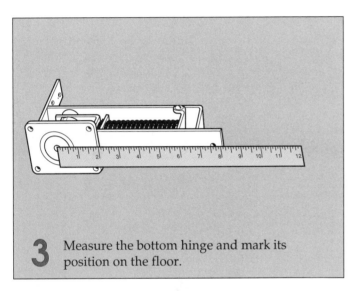

3 Measure the bottom hinge and mark its position on the floor.

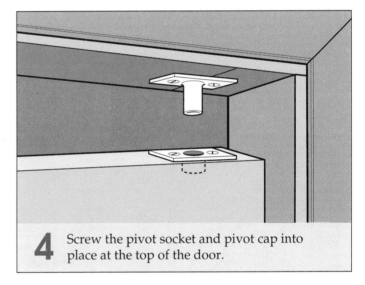

4 Screw the pivot socket and pivot cap into place at the top of the door.

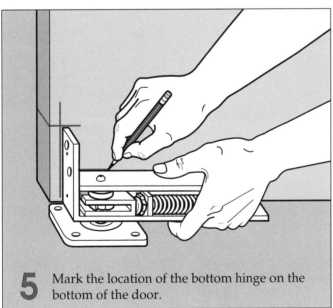

5 Mark the location of the bottom hinge on the bottom of the door.

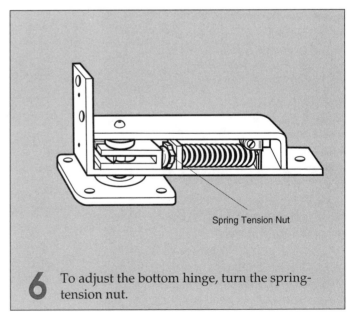

Spring Tension Nut

6 To adjust the bottom hinge, turn the spring-tension nut.

Installing Sliding Doors

Sliding doors (sometimes called patio doors) can make a wonderful addition to nearly any room because they let in so much light. You will have to be careful when installing them, however, because weather proofing is essential. Also, the units are quite heavy, so line up some help during the installation.

1 Making the Rough Opening. Lay out the door's rough opening according to the dimensions suggested by the manufacturer. An existing stud may have to be moved or new ones added.

2 Building the Header. Cut two lengths of header lumber, using the chart on page 55 to determine the proper width and thickness to use. Nail the two pieces of header lumber together with 16d nails, with a piece of 1/2-inch plywood between them as a spacer. The overall thickness of the header should match the width of the wall studs.

3 Installing the Header. In most home construction, the header should be 6 feet 10 1/2 inches from the subfloor. Position the header at this height between regular studs. Nail through the studs into each end of the header. You can also hang the header on metal brackets if you prefer; these are available at most building supply stores.

4 Installing Trimmer Studs. Cut trimmers to fit snugly between the soleplate and the header. Nail them to the regular studs with 10d nails. If the rough opening is unusually large, double the trimmers on both sides of the opening to provide extra support for the header; consult local building codes. If necessary, cut the sole-plate away from the rough opening, then nail exterior sheathing to the outside of the exposed framing.

5 Positioning the Door. If the door frame is unassembled, follow assembly instructions pro-

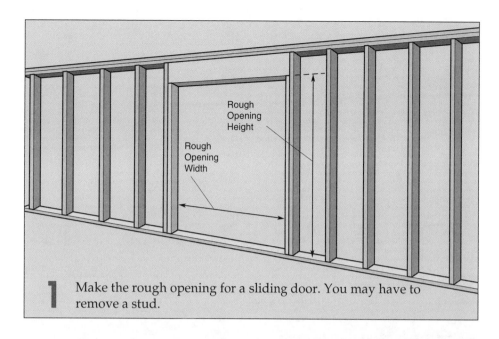

1 Make the rough opening for a sliding door. You may have to remove a stud.

Rough Opening Height

Rough Opening Width

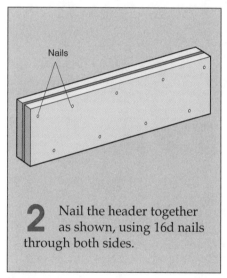

Nails

2 Nail the header together as shown, using 16d nails through both sides.

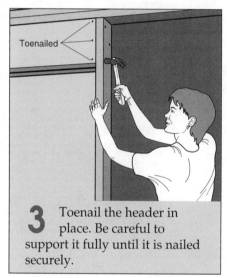

Toenailed

3 Toenail the header in place. Be careful to support it fully until it is nailed securely.

Trimmer Stud

4 Install a trimmer stud on both ends of the header to support it, and nail the stud into place.

Sill

5 Caulk beneath the door sill before setting it into place. Then level it carefully.

C-clamp

6 Use a C-clamp to hold the door flanges tightly to the wall, then screw the jambs to the framing.

vided by the manufacturer. Usually, the door unit is placed into the rough opening from the outside of the house. To provide a tight seal between the door sill and the floor, run caulk across the underside of the sill before setting the unit into place. If the sill is to rest on concrete, use sill sealer insulation beneath it. In either case, make sure the sill is level.

6 **Securing the Frame.** Wide vinyl flanges, which provide flashing, are ordinarily used at head and side jambs. They are not intended to be nailing flanges.

To hold the frame in place after setting it into the rough opening, use C-clamps—they will also help to draw the flanges tight against the sheathing. Check the jambs for plumb, and double-check the sill for level. Note that side jambs usually have predrilled holes for installation screws. Shim between the jambs and the framing at these points and drive the screws into place, but be sure to keep the jambs plumb as you go.

7 **Positioning the Fixed Panel.** Some sliding door units have two sliding panels, while others feature a sliding panel and a fixed panel. To install the fixed panel, lift it into place between the head and sill, and in the outer channel of both. Push the panel against the side jamb, using blocks to wedge it into place. Be careful, though, applying too much pressure will crack the glass.

8 **Securing the Fixed Panel.** Adjust the panel until you can install the parting stop in the head jamb. At the sill, secure the panel by screwing into it through the stationary sill filler.

9 **Installing the Operating Panel.** Now, place the operating panel into place on the sill. Tip the door in at the top and slide it to the closed position. Check the

7 Wedge the fixed panel into place temporarily. Exerting too much pressure will crack the glass.

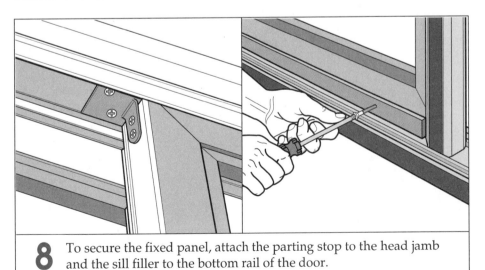

8 To secure the fixed panel, attach the parting stop to the head jamb and the sill filler to the bottom rail of the door.

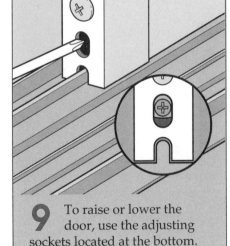

9 To raise or lower the door, use the adjusting sockets located at the bottom.

door by sliding it back and forth. If it sticks, binds, or is not square with the frame, locate two adjustment sockets on the inside bottom rail of the panel and unscrew the caps. Then insert a screwdriver and turn to raise or lower the door. Replace the caps and test the door.

10 **Adjust the Latch.** The latch in the panel must engage the keeper bracket on the jamb.

If it does not, turn the adjusting screw to move the latch in or out as necessary.

11 **Caulking and Sealing the Door.** To finish the job, caulk and weatherstrip the door. Before

closing up the inside of the wall, however, fill in any exposed framing cavities with insulation, and use spray-foam insulation to seal any cracks between the wall framing and the door jambs.

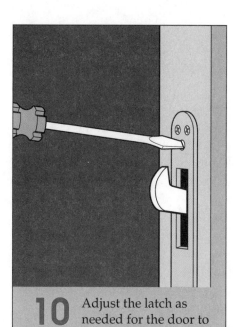

10 Adjust the latch as needed for the door to close and lock properly.

11 Sliding doors must be weatherproofed carefully. Use the recommended head flashing and good quality caulk.

Installing Cafe Swinging Doors

Smaller cafe-type swinging doors are installed in pairs. They are hung on gravity-pivot hinges, which allow the weight of the doors to swing them shut. Each hinge consists of a jamb socket screwed to a side jamb and a pivot mounted on the top or bottom of the door. Notches in the bottom hinge fit together to hold the door open.

To install cafe-type swinging doors, mount the bottom jamb socket, screw the pivots to the top and bottom of the door, and slip the door into the bottom socket. Then fit the top jamb socket over the top pivot and screw the socket to the jamb.

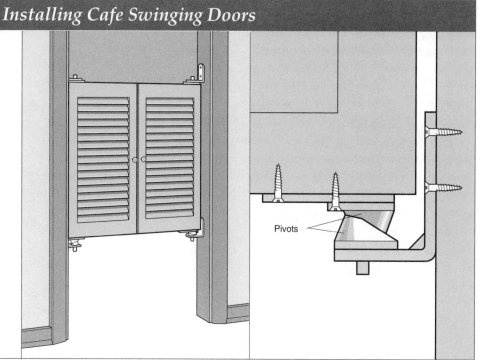

Door Repairs

Even your best installation efforts will sometimes result in a door that, for some reason or other, doesn't quite fit. Make any necessary alterations and repairs as soon as possible; a misfitting or misaligned door can damage the jamb and the door itself, not to mention the greater air infiltration that occurs around it.

Binding is a common problem with hinged doors. Use the following technique to free a binding door:

■ If the door is binding near the top or bottom of the latch edge, first be sure the screws holding the hinges to the jamb are tight. If they are, shim one of the hinges with cardboard, placed behind the hinge leaf connected to the jamb. Shim the top hinge to free a bind near the bottom and the bottom hinge for a bind near the top.

■ If the top or bottom of the door binds, close the door as far as possible to determine where the bind is occurring. Lightly mark the high spots. If the bind is at the top, open the door partway and plane or sand down the high spots, working from the edges to the center of the door to avoid splintering the end grain.

■ If material must be removed from the hinge side or bottom edge, the door will have to be taken down for planing. To do this, first close the door as far as possible, then work a pry bar between the hinge pin and top of the hinge, and tap it loose with a hammer. Replace each of the pins in the hinge leaf fastened to the jamb immediately after removing the door to avoid losing them.

■ Stand the door on its edge with one end in a corner and straddle the other end. Plane down the high spots on the hinge edge with a jack plane. Use a block plane to remove excess wood from the bottom edge. Always plane from the ends of the door to the center.

Freeing a Binding Hinged Door

If the door is binding near the top or bottom of the latch edge of the door, you can shim the hinges with cardboard.

To remove the door for planing work a pry bar between the hinge pin and the top of the hinge, and tap it loose with a hammer.

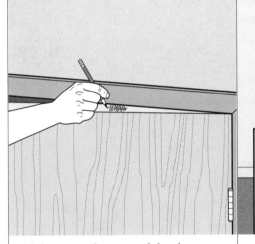

If the top or bottom of the door binds, determine where the bind is occurring and mark the spots.

Plane down the high spots on the hinge edge with a jack plane.

Fixing a Warped Door

A perfectly good door can be practically unserviceable if it becomes warped or bowed. For a door that is bowed in the middle, try straightening it with weights. Lay it across a pair of sawhorses, with the bulge up, and place bricks or similar heavy objects in the center until the force of the weight straightens the door.

If the door is just slightly out of line, it may be possible to move the door stop to conform with the door. If the stop is not set into, or part of, the jamb, pry it loose. Close the door, then move the stop to the correct position on the door and nail it in place.

Replacing Thresholds

All exterior doors should have a threshold to provide a durable transition into the house. Combined with weatherstripping, the threshold also helps to keep out drafts and insects.

These are several common types of replacement thresholds. Most combine an aluminum base with some form of flexible weatherstripping.

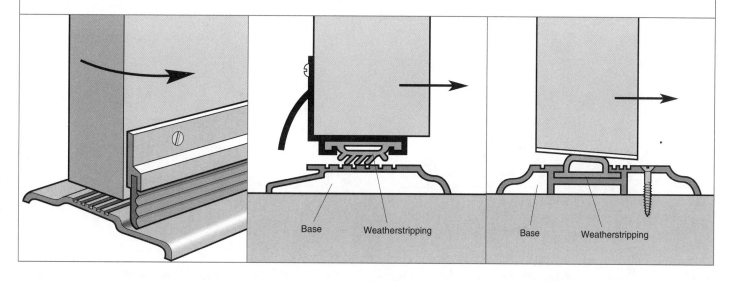

Base   Weatherstripping

Base   Weatherstripping

Repairing the Strike & Latch

A latch and strike plate that do not quite match up will prevent any door from closing properly. This problem can be handled with a few adjustments.

1. First, check to see which edge of the strike plate the latch is hitting. If only a minor adjustment is necessary, remove the strike plate, put it in a vise, and file down the offending edge. Or lengthen the mortise and move the strike plate up or down as needed for a correct fit.

2. If the door does not close far enough for the latch to engage the strike plate, the door's stop must be moved. (This procedure also works well for doors that rattle while closed.) Pry off the stop from the jambs. Place a scrap of wood between the pry bar and the jamb to prevent damage. After the stop is removed, close the door and make a line on the jamb to indicate where the edge of the stop should be. Then reposition the stop along this line. Finish by painting or staining the area left exposed when stops were moved.

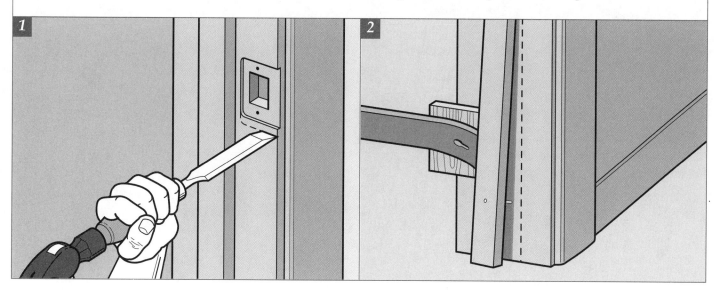

In cold climates, a storm door provides an extra layer of protection against air infiltration, and protects the main door from the weather. In hot weather, the glazing can be replaced with a screen to provide extra ventilation when the main door is open. Storm doors are typically made of aluminum, and consist of a door and an integral mounting flange.

Installation is straightforward. Once you've located a door unit to fit the opening around your existing door, screw the door's mounting flange directly to the existing casing. Check the door as you go to make sure it stays squarely within the mounting flange. Door closing hardware can be attached after the door is in place.

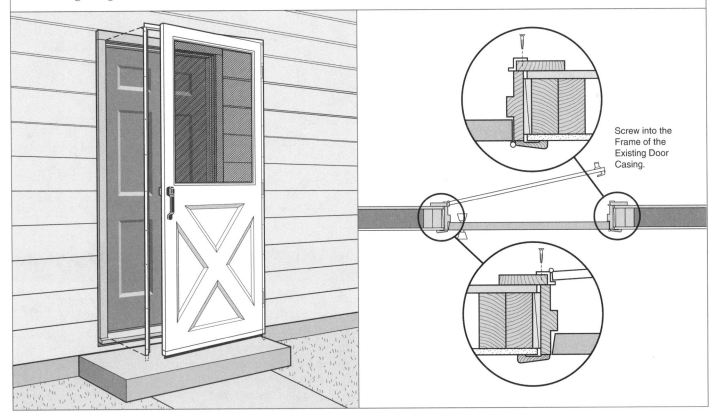

Screw into the Frame of the Existing Door Casing.

Repairing Sliding Doors

These heavy, glass exterior doors slide on rollers mounted on the bottom of the door frame. Most problems are caused by dirt that collects on the track in which the door slides. Therefore, many problems can be avoided by keeping the track clean. After each cleaning, puff powdered graphite onto the track or apply paraffin to keep the door running smoothly.

A bent track can also cause a door to bind. This problem can often be solved by tapping out the bend with a hammer and wooden block.

If a door is not sliding squarely on its rollers, check to see if the door's movable sash is square with the track. If it is out of alignment, adjust the rollers up or down by locating the access plug near the bottom of the door. Turn the plug's screw clockwise to raise the rollers, counterclockwise to lower them.

Repairing Bypass Doors

When bypass doors act up, one of three things has usually happened. The screws holding the roller brackets may have come loose, one of the rollers may have jumped the track, or the floor door guides may have become bent.

Tightening the screws holding the roller brackets in place, lifting the roller back on track again, and straightening or replacing the floor door guides will get the problem door rolling properly again.

S K Y L I G H T S

Skylights are a versatile and economical way to bring natural sunlight to wherever it is needed. Skylights can be as long as a room, or as small as 18 inches square. They may be operable (called ventilating skylights) or inoperable (called fixed skylights).

Choosing a Location

Skylights can be an asset to a home in many ways. They can be a major source of solar heat gain, for one. Generous amounts of sunlight are admitted into the living space; the sunlight is then converted into heat as it strikes the interior surfaces. The resulting energy savings can be substantial. In addition, skylights can make any room feel light and airy even on gloomy days. They allow sunlight to penetrate deep into a room.

Skylights and windows can reinforce one another to provide a balanced influx of luxurious sunlight all year long. In a room where there are already windows on one wall, place the skylight so that its light balances the window light.

For the most light, place a skylight where it has southern exposure. Generally, it is best to avoid skylights facing west because they can heat up too much in the summer. A skylight facing east is ideal for introducing extra light into kitchens and breakfast areas. Skylights facing north typically lose more heat than they gain, but they also admit a very even, glare-free light that many people enjoy. Remember that direct light can fade fabrics; use a diffuser if this is a potential problem in your house.

For energy efficiency and privacy factors, shutters or insulated panels can be installed to close off a skylight.

Although the interior of the house is important when deciding where to place a skylight, the exterior needs to be considered as well. Ideally, the skylight should harmonize with the outside of the home. In addition, check for nearby tree limbs that could fall off or bob in the wind, damaging a skylight. Prune them before the skylight is installed. Plastic glazing may be a wiser choice than glass when the skylight is near trees, in high-vandalism areas, or in other situations where the window could be damaged.

Essential Parts of a Skylight

Skylights are glazed either with glass or with various plastics. A glass skylight is always flat, while plastic skylights usually are domed. In cold climates, either type of glazing should be doubled, with an airspace between, to minimize heat loss and reduce condensation problems. Glass should be tempered or wired for safety. Options include tinted glass to reduce glare, reflective glass to limit heat gain, or frosted glass for privacy. You can also get low-e or argon-filled glazing from some manufacturers for extra energy efficiency. Some ventilating skylights can even be fitted with motorized controls so you can open and close them from a wall switch or remote control.

The basic structure of a skylight varies. Many skylights rest on a wood frame, called a curb, that lifts the skylight above the plane of the roof. The curb is generally assembled by the homeowner from standard lumber. Metal flashing protects the curb from water infiltration. Other skylights, sometimes called "curbless" skylights, are manufactured to be attached directly to the roof, instead of to a curb. These units are sometimes easier to install because they include integral flashing—more on that later.

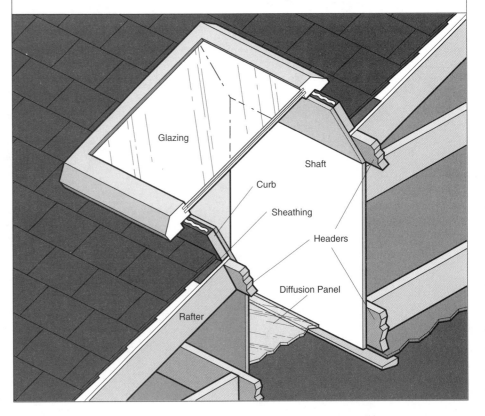

Choosing a Location. In a room that has windows only on one wall, place the skylight to bring light deep into the room and to reduce glare.

What Kind of Roof Do You Have?

Pitched roofs can be covered with all sorts of materials. Flat or low-pitched roofs are often covered with roofing felt built up in layers and topped with gravel. A skylight can be installed in either type of roof, but one covered with slate, tile, or metal makes the job tricky. These materials must be cut with specialized tools, and the skylight must be waterproofed with considerable care. If you have this kind of a roof, contact a local builder or a contractor for specific recommendations. Luckily, most roofs are covered with wood, asphalt or fiberglass shingles. These are the easiest in which to install a skylight.

Next, check the framing in the attic. You must be very careful in unfinished attics because walking across exposed joists is tough. Never step directly on insulation, which is almost always supported by drywall alone and will not support much weight. The safest thing to do is lay boards or plywood panels at right angles to the joists to serve as a catwalk.

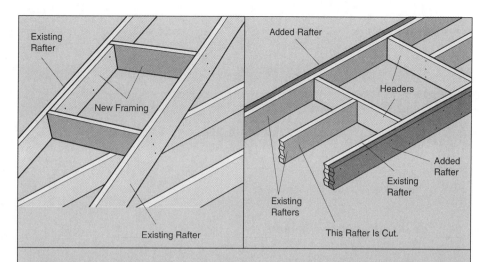

What Kind of Roof Do You Have? If the skylight will fit between rafters, box in the opening to fit the skylight dimensions between the rafters (left). Headers that are plumb to the floor and on the diagonal on the rafter are trickier to install. If rafters must be cut to accommodate a large skylight (right), double the rafters on either side of the opening and install headers to support the ends of the cut rafter. Nail headers the same size as the rafters to the side rafters.

Note distances between rafters and ceiling joists—most skylight units are designed to fit a 24-inch spacing or multiples of that dimension. For larger skylights or for a roof that has 16-inch on-center construction, rafters and joists must sometimes be cut to accommodate the skylight.

Consult an architect or engineer and work from professionally prepared plans to cut roof trusses. Trusses must not be cut without professional advice. In the case of unusually large skylights, the headers may have to be doubled, but again, consult an architect or engineer.

Before You Begin

Decide whether to work from the inside out—framing the ceiling opening and building the shaft before cutting into the roof—or to work from the roof in, as in "Installing Factory Built Skylights" on the next page. Whichever method, plan to cut through the roof early in the day and close it up the same day—that way the chance of water damage from a sudden weather change is mini-mized. To install a skylight, a helper may be needed to transport the unit up to the roof and to set it in place.

Once the skylight is in place, cut through the ceiling and construct a plywood or drywall shaft. Plywood or drywall usually is easiest to install piece by piece. It is nailed one by one to the framing of the shaft. The shaft can be installed several ways. If the light is desired directly under the roof opening, build an angled box. Or the shaft itself can be tilted so that it is perpendicular to the roof, angling the light. To create a lighted area in the room that is bigger than the skylight itself, splay the sides of the shaft, somewhat like a pyramid with its top lopped off. To do this, the opening in the ceiling will have to be larger.

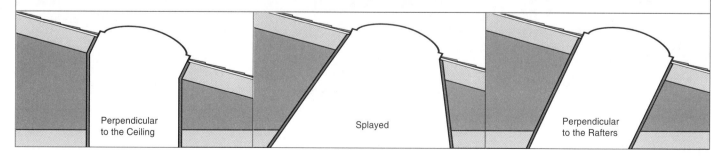

Perpendicular to the Ceiling

Splayed

Perpendicular to the Rafters

Installing Factory Built Skylights

Before cutting into the roof, check the layout instructions that come with most skylights. They will give specific dimensions for the curb and other elements of the job. Remember that the curb must fit the skylight, and the roof opening must fit the curb, so use these dimensions as your guide.

1 Locating the Roof Opening. Drive two nails from inside the attic along the rafter and up through the sheathing. These nails will serve as marks for one side of the square to be cut from the outside. (Before cutting anything, however, check the area for wiring and water lines.) If rafters will have to be cut, either do it now or wait until the sheathing is opened. To prevent sags or breaks in the rafters, brace them to the ceiling joists below before sawing.

2 Removing Shingles. With an ordinary garden spade, carefully pop up as many courses of shingles as necessary to clear the area where the skylight will be located. Be sure to cut back the shingles and the underlying roofing felt at least 8 inches around the intended opening.

3 Cutting the Roof Opening. Using the nails driven from the inside as reference points, lay out the exact opening for the roof cutout. Cut the roof opening 3/4 inches wider and higher than the outside dimensions of the skylight, using a circular saw or saber saw. Nail headers in place.

4 Locating the Corners. Mark the four corners of the shaft opening on the now-exposed ceiling by using a level as a plumb guide. Drive nails down through these points to serve as guides for a later cut.

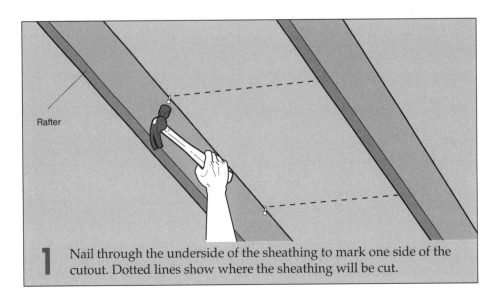

1 Nail through the underside of the sheathing to mark one side of the cutout. Dotted lines show where the sheathing will be cut.

Rafter

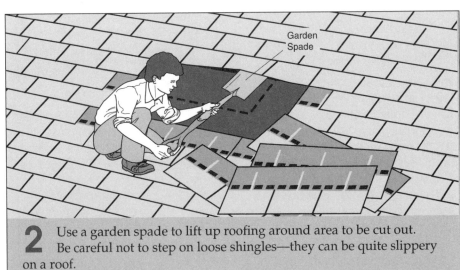

2 Use a garden spade to lift up roofing around area to be cut out. Be careful not to step on loose shingles—they can be quite slippery on a roof.

Garden Spade

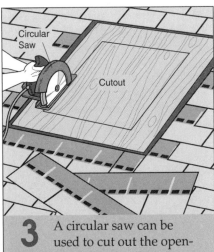

Circular Saw

Cutout

3 A circular saw can be used to cut out the opening through the sheathing in the roof. Be sure to have a firm footing on the roof before operating a power tool.

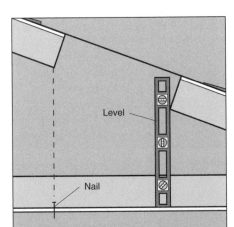

Level

Nail

4 Use a level to locate the corners for the shaft down through the ceiling. All measurements when installing skylights must be square.

5 Building the Curb. If the skylight to be installed requires a curb—a simple box made of 2x4s or 2x6s and placed around the roof opening to serve as a mounting base—build it to match the opening. Its inside dimensions should be the same as the hole in the roof. Be sure the corners are square.

6 Installing the Curb. Nail the curb securely to the roof. Bed it in roof cement to provide an extra measure of sealing.

7 Sealing the Curb. With some skylights, an angled strip of wood, called a cant strip, may be required around the curb. Bedded in roof cement and angled to shed water, it serves as an additional barrier against water infiltration. In most skylight installations, however, it is not required.

8 Flashing the Curb. Replace some of the old roofing felt removed earlier so that it continues up the side of the curb. Assemble the flashing around the curb. Some skylights are manufactured with custom-made flashing; generally, there will be a head flashing, bottom flashing, and two pieces of side flashing. After the flashing is in place, replace the shingles and add another coat of cement to seal the curb's edge.

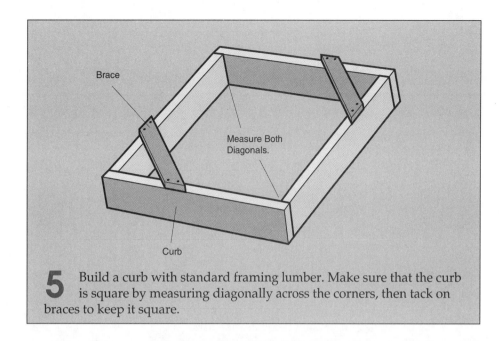

Brace

Measure Both Diagonals.

Curb

5 Build a curb with standard framing lumber. Make sure that the curb is square by measuring diagonally across the corners, then tack on braces to keep it square.

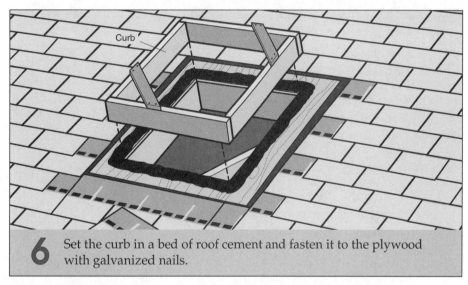

Curb

6 Set the curb in a bed of roof cement and fasten it to the plywood with galvanized nails.

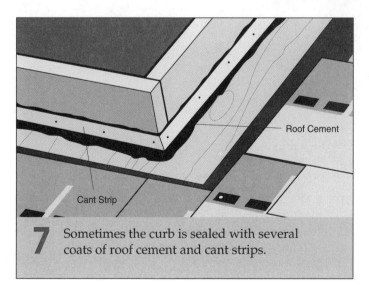

Roof Cement

Cant Strip

7 Sometimes the curb is sealed with several coats of roof cement and cant strips.

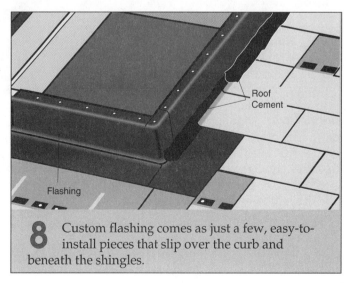

Roof Cement

Flashing

8 Custom flashing comes as just a few, easy-to-install pieces that slip over the curb and beneath the shingles.

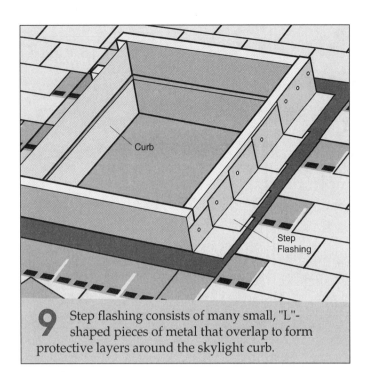

9 Step flashing consists of many small, "L"-shaped pieces of metal that overlap to form protective layers around the skylight curb.

10 Temporarily nailing the skylight in place will allow the next step—opening up the ceiling.

9 **Step-flashing the Curb.**
Some types of skylights require multiple courses of flashing, called step flashing. Step flashing is made of galvanized metal or copper. It can be made, but can also be purchased at a reasonable price at most building supply stores. Sizes should run at least 3 inches up the curb. Be careful to overlap the pieces to match existing shingle exposure. Basically, each piece of step flashing is installed as the roof shingles are replaced. The top of each flashing piece is nailed to the curb. Dab a bit of roof cement over each nail head to seal it.

10 **Reinstalling the Shingles.**
Working up the roof from the lowest course removed, nail the shingles in place, taking care to keep the courses even for best appearance. After completing this step, temporarily nail the skylight in place—you may have to remove it later while you're working on the skylight shaft, but you don't want it to blow off the roof in the meantime.

11 **Cutting the Ceiling.** With the skylight temporarily secured on the roof, it's time to open up the ceiling and build the

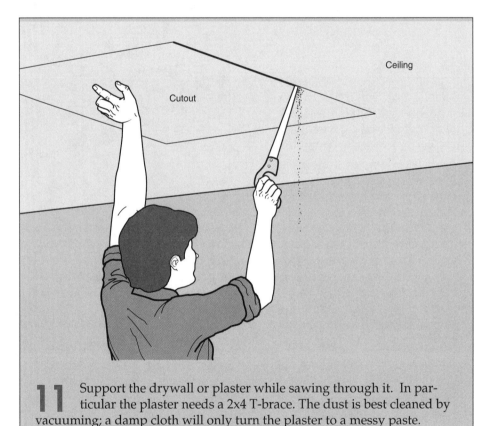

11 Support the drywall or plaster while sawing through it. In particular the plaster needs a 2x4 T-brace. The dust is best cleaned by vacuuming; a damp cloth will only turn the plaster to a messy paste.

skylight shaft. To open the ceiling, use a keyhole saw or reciprocating saw. Lay plastic sheeting below to catch the dust created by cutting through the drywall or plaster. Be sure to wear goggles and a dust mask. Drywall can be supported with one hand while sawing (if using a keyhole saw), but plaster is heavier and should be supported with a 2x4 T-brace wedged against the floor.

12 **Framing the Shaft.** Frame between joists, if necessary, and be sure to support the ends of any rafters you had to cut by framing in a doubled header, as with the rafters. Frame the walls of the shaft to support drywall or other finish shaft surfaces.

13 **Finishing the Shaft.** Installing finished surfaces of the shaft requires careful figuring. It might be wise to experiment with cardboard templates before cutting plywood or drywall to fit. Secure drywall to the framing and tape as usual. If you prefer a shaft made of plywood, then secure it to the framing and caulk the corners prior to painting. Then make a trip to the attic to check the insulation. Batts and blankets should fit snugly around the base of the light shaft. Insulate the shaft, as well.

14 **Fastening the Skylight to the Curb.** First spread clear silicone sealant on the curb's top edge, and press the skylight into place. Secure the skylight to the curb with galvanized screws. Some skylights (called self-flashing skylights) do not need a curb. Instead, they are integral units that include a flashing apron. If using a self-flashing skylight, tuck the apron under the top and sides of the roofing, but let it overlap the down-roof shingles.

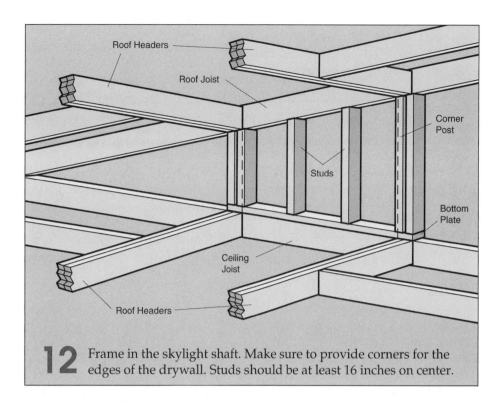

12 Frame in the skylight shaft. Make sure to provide corners for the edges of the drywall. Studs should be at least 16 inches on center.

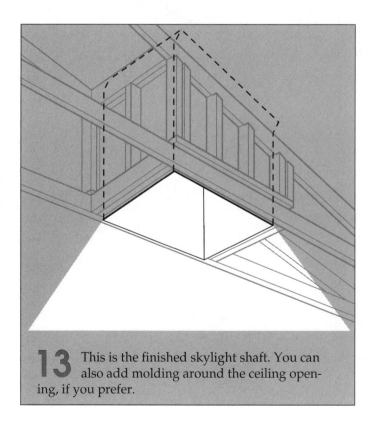

13 This is the finished skylight shaft. You can also add molding around the ceiling opening, if you prefer.

14 Install a skylight by bedding it in silicone sealant. Use galvanized flat head screws to attach it to the curb.

Building a Skylight

Be assured when buying a manufactured skylight that much thought has gone into its design. You can, however, build your own skylight. Such a project is more time consuming than buying a manufactured design, but it will generally turn out to be less expensive. Another advantage is that the skylight can be made the precise size needed—manufactured skylights are available in standard sizes that may not suit every situation.

When it comes to picking glazing for a skylight, the most important point to remember is never use standard window glass. Such glass is not strong enough for overhead use. When damaged, it breaks into razor-sharp shards that could be deadly to anyone unlucky enough to be standing below. Instead, use tempered glass, wired safety glass, or an exterior-grade plastic. Tempered glass and wired glass cannot be cut on site; each must be special-ordered from a glass company to the exact size. Plastic is more likely to scratch, and allowances are needed for it to expand and contract. Cutting techniques for plastic depend on the type and thickness; check with the supplier for cutting instructions.

The key to success when building a skylight is to be meticulous with flashing and caulking against the weather.

1 **Building the Curb.** After determining the size of the skylight, the first step is to build the curb out of straight 2x6 lumber. After the curb is nailed together, add temporary corner braces to keep it square until installing it on the roof. Make the braces out of scrap wood and tack them into place so you can pull the nails easily later on.

2 **Marking the Flashing.** Mark a pattern on strips of 10-inch wide aluminum flashing, using dashed lines to represent folds and solid lines to represent cuts. Flashing typically comes in a roll. You may want to duplicate your layout onto a full-size paper pattern. By cutting and folding the paper pattern according to your layout, you can check the accuracy of your work. For an extra measure of protection against leaks, you can include a "hemmed" edge along the length of both side flashings. To make it, simply turn up the flashing edge and bend it back over the flashing. Do not fold it completely flat, however.

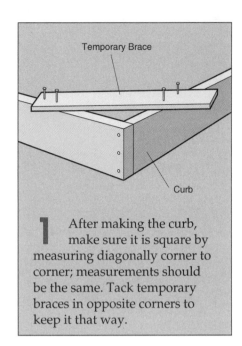

1 After making the curb, make sure it is square by measuring diagonally corner to corner; measurements should be the same. Tack temporary braces in opposite corners to keep it that way.

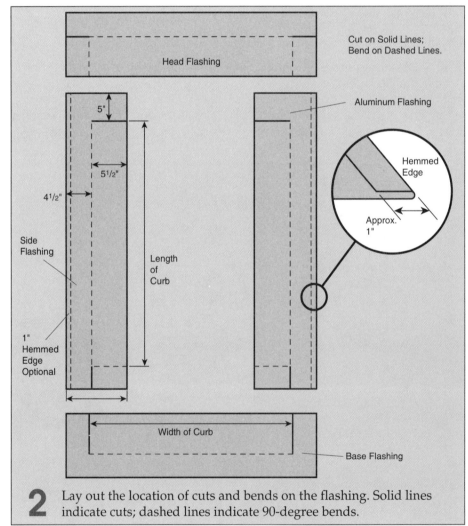

2 Lay out the location of cuts and bends on the flashing. Solid lines indicate cuts; dashed lines indicate 90-degree bends.

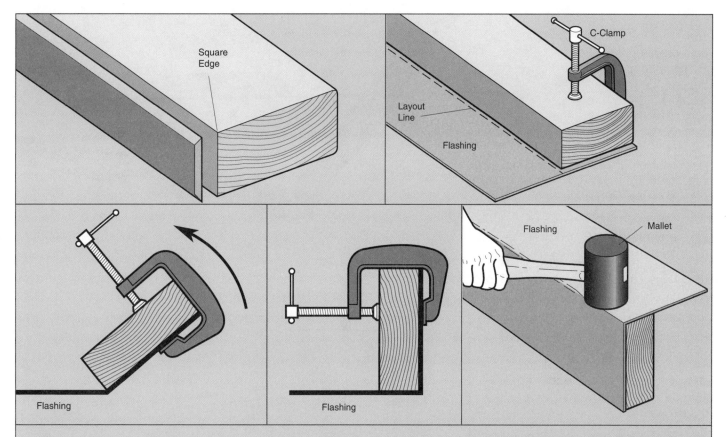

3 Trim off the edge of a 2x6 with a table saw; it should be as long as the longest piece of flashing. Use several clamps to hold the 2x6 against a layout line. Pivot the 2x6 upward to bend the flashing. Use a rubber mallet to complete the bend; you may have to remove the clamps first.

3 Bending the Flashing.

To bend flashing, trim one 2x6 to square up the edges. Clamp the 2x6 along a dashed layout line, then lift up on the lumber so that one edge pivots on the line. Then turn the lumber on edge and use a rubber mallet to complete the bend. To cut flashing, use tin snips, but be careful because the cut edges and corners will be sharp. Wear leather gloves to protect your hands.

4 Assembling the Flashing.

After bending and cutting the flashing, test-fit it against the curb. The bottom flashing goes in first, then the side flashing, and lastly the head flashing. This order is important so that each piece overlaps the one below it. The hemmed

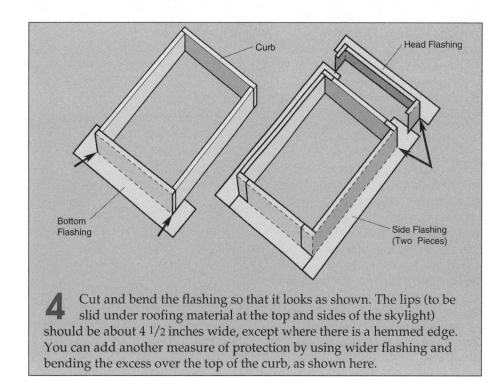

4 Cut and bend the flashing so that it looks as shown. The lips (to be slid under roofing material at the top and sides of the skylight) should be about 4 1/2 inches wide, except where there is a hemmed edge. You can add another measure of protection by using wider flashing and bending the excess over the top of the curb, as shown here.

edge on the side flashings is an additional barrier to prevent water from slipping past and reaching the sheathing. With this flashing system, the chance for leakage is greatest at the four points indicated by arrows. This is where the pieces of flashing overlap in such a way as to leave a single weak point at each location. Be particularly careful to seal these areas with high-quality silicone sealant while assembling the flashing.

5   **Installing the Curb.** Bed the curb in silicone sealant and toenail it into place over the hole in the roof. Remove any braces from the curb and seal the base with roof cement. Cut spacer strips to fit around of the curb. The strips should be about 1/2-inch wide and 1/4-inch thicker than the glazing. Nail the strips around the outer edge of the curb with galvanized casing or finish nails.

6   **Preparing the Angle Stock.** Aluminum angle stock is used to hold down the glazing. Cut four pieces of 3-inch by 3-inch angle stock. Drill and countersink each piece, as shown. Use 2-inch #8 galvanized wood screws on top and 1-inch screws on the sides. Space side holes 9 inches apart and 1/2-inch from the bottom of the angle.

7   **Adding the Glazing.** Lay a bead of silicone sealant on the curb 1/2 inch from the inside edge, then lay the glazing on top, position it evenly on the curb, and gently press it into the silicone. You may want to nail a couple of small finish nails into the curb just inside the bottom spacer strips; they will serve as stops to keep the glazing from sliding downward. The nails can be left in place permanently. There should be at least 1/8 inch of clearance between the edge of the glazing and the spacer strip; this will allow for the necessary expansion and contraction.

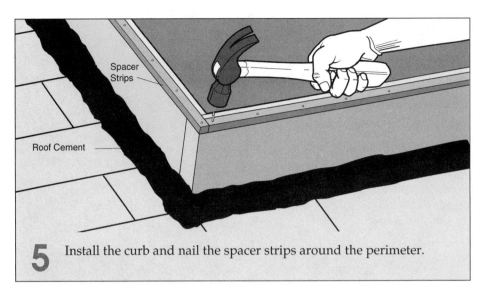

5   Install the curb and nail the spacer strips around the perimeter.

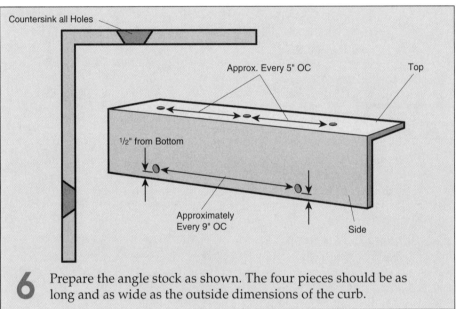

6   Prepare the angle stock as shown. The four pieces should be as long and as wide as the outside dimensions of the curb.

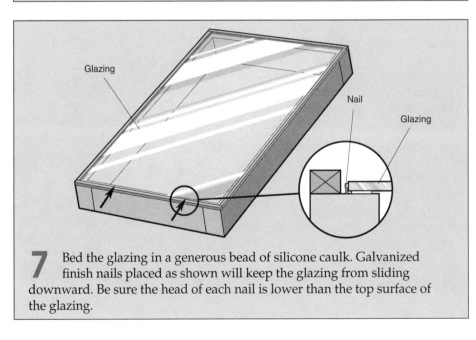

7   Bed the glazing in a generous bead of silicone caulk. Galvanized finish nails placed as shown will keep the glazing from sliding downward. Be sure the head of each nail is lower than the top surface of the glazing.

8 **Installing the Angles.** Install the angles with the side pieces lapping over the top and bottom ones to give the skylight a natural run-off.

9 **Caulking.** Place a bead of silicone caulk on the glazing so that each angle will squeeze it against the glazing for a tight seal. Screw each angle in place. Tool all caulk seams to push the caulk into the joints and smooth it. Cover all exposed screw heads with silicone caulk as well.

10 **Completing the Skylight.** The completed skylight is an interlocking assembly of parts designed to shed water. You should check the integrity of all caulked seams each year.

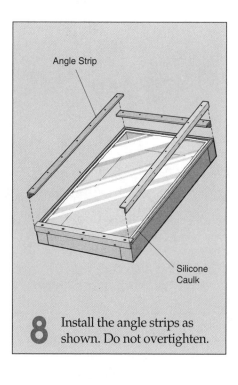

Angle Strip

Silicone Caulk

8 Install the angle strips as shown. Do not overtighten.

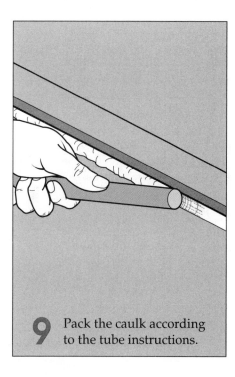

9 Pack the caulk according to the tube instructions.

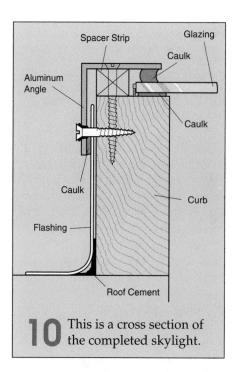

Spacer Strip

Glazing

Caulk

Aluminum Angle

Caulk

Caulk

Curb

Caulk

Flashing

Roof Cement

10 This is a cross section of the completed skylight.

Working with Plastic Glazing

If you will be using plastic glazing on your skylight, here's how to work with the material.

■ When cutting 1/4-inch plastic glazing, use a blade with fourteen teeth per inch. To cut a straight line, clamp a straightedge to the sheet as a guide. For circular saws and table saws, use the type of cross-cut blade recommended for finish cuts on veneer plywood.

■ Hold the material firmly and do not force-feed it. Also, do not remove the paper backing when cutting.

■ When drilling plastic glazing, always back up the material with a block of wood and use a drill bit that is sharp. For small holes, highest speed is best. When the bit is about to come through the far side, slow down to avoid chipping.

■ When drilling holes in the side of the plastic glazing box, allow for the expansion and contraction of the plas-tic glazing by drilling holes 1/16-inch oversize for every foot on the side. Keep at least 1/4-inch of material from the circumference of the drill hole to the edge of the piece.

■ To prepare the edge for gluing, first scrape the edge with the back of a hacksaw blade or sand it down with 80-grit sandpaper. After the saw marks are gone, switch to 150-grit wet or dry paper to produce a clean, satin finish.

■ There are two types of cement for plastic glazing: capillary cement and thickened cement. Be very careful with either type and avoid the vapors as much as possible. Capillary cement can be used only with general purpose plastic glazing and is applied with a special needle. The joint must be kept horizontal to allow the cement to flow properly.

Thickened cement is applied differently. After checking for a proper fit, add a small bead of cement to one piece. Join the two pieces together and clamp until set.

Maintenance & Repair

When a skylight has been installed properly, it should be fairly trouble-free, except for needing minor, periodic maintenance. If you notice any water stains around the skylight well, however, or drips coming from the ceiling area around the skylight, investigate the problem immediately.

Condensation Problems

Before you head up to investigate the roof, see if the "leakage" is actually condensation. When warm, moist air comes into contact with a cool surface, moisture may be deposited on the surface in a process called condensation. This is because warm air can hold more moisture than cool air. Because the glazing of skylights (and windows) is usually the coolest part of a wall, that's where you generally see condensation. Modest amounts of moisture aren't a problem, but heavy condensation will run down the skylight and leak onto surrounding surfaces. Tightly sealed, energy efficient homes are more prone to

condensation problems because moisture generated by showers, cooking, or other sources can't escape as it might in an older, less tightly-sealed house.

To check for condensation, examine the inside surface of the glazing when you first notice drips. If the surface is covered with small water droplets, that problem is probably condensation. To eliminate condensation problems, first try to reduce the moisture levels inside the house by turning on kitchen or bathroom ventilating fans when those rooms are being used. Secondly, you can add another layer of glazing to the inside surface of the skylight. This will reduce the temperature difference between the skylight glazing and the room.

Leakage Problems

Condensation can occur whether or not it is raining, but if there's a leak, you will notice it during or just after a rain. Leaks are notoriously difficult to track down, though there are some common sources you should always check.

Leaves and other debris can collect around a skylight, causing water to back up and leak beneath the shingles. The solution is simple: once a year, brush away the debris. Another source of leakage is poorly installed or deteriorating flashing. Examine all the flashing around the skylight for rust or damage, and replace faulty flashing as needed. This may involve removing shingles around the immediate area. Minor problems can sometimes be solved temporarily by applying roofing sealant to the affected area. While you're at it, dab some sealant over the heads of any exposed nails. Water leakage may also be due to problems in the roofing above the skylight—damaged shingles, perhaps, or deteriorating flashing around a plumbing vent. Water from such sources may be trickling down a rafter until it reaches the skylight

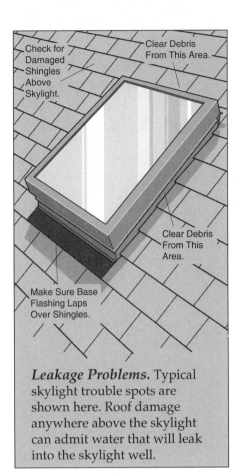

Leakage Problems. Typical skylight trouble spots are shown here. Roof damage anywhere above the skylight can admit water that will leak into the skylight well.

framing. Check for this from the attic side of the roof, and look for brownish stains on rafters or on the underside of the sheathing.

Replacing Damaged Glazing

Unfortunately, cracked or broken skylight glazing isn't something that can be repaired easily. Many commercial skylights, particularly those with plastic glazing, are sealed units—to replace the glazing, you have to replace the entire skylight. Curb-mounted skylights are generally the easiest to remove and replace. In any case, check with the skylight manufacturer to see if replacement glazing is available.

Wood Stops

Clear, Rigid Plastic

Condensation Problems. By adding a layer of glazing inside the skylight well, you can reduce condensation problems. The additional glazing traps an insulating layer of air beneath the existing skylight.

Apron The piece of trim at the bottom of a window, below the stool.

Butt joint A joint in which a square-cut piece of wood is attached to the end or face of a second piece.

Bypass doors Lightweight wood interior doors that hang from rollers that slide in a track attached to the head jamb.

Cant strip An angled strip of wood installed at the perimeter of a skylight as extra protection against water infiltration.

Capillary cement Adhesive designed for use with general purpose plastic glazing and applied with a special needle.

Casing The trim that lines the inside and outside of a doorway or window frame.

Caulk A soft compound for sealing joints against leaks (of water, air, and noise). It may be silicone, neoprene, or one of a variety of other synthetic compounds.

Clad wood window A composite window made of wood and encased by vinyl; requires little maintenance and is energy-efficient.

Condensation Moisture that forms when warm, moist air comes into contact with a cool surface. Usually found on windows and skylights, condensation is only a problem in heavy amounts, when it can lead to leaks.

Cripple stud The shortened stud found above a doorway or window and below a window; provides structural support and a nailing surface for drywall.

Curb The wooden frame that elevates a skylight above the plane of the roof.

Diffuser A translucent plastic panel placed under a light fixture or skylight to admit light, while masking what is above.

Double-glazed window A window consisting of two panes of glass separated by an airspace; the air provides most of the insulating capability.

Flanged window A window that is manufactured with a perimeter nailing flange to facilitate installation.

Flashing Strips of thin metal attached to the junction of the roof and skylight to prevent leaks.

Galvanizing To coat a metal with a thin layer of zinc to prevent rust. Galvanized nails are ideal for installing skylights, windows, and exterior doors because of their superior strength and corrosion-resistance.

Glazier's points Small clips used with glazing compound to secure replacement glass in the sash.

Glazing Clear coating or film used to reduce the amount of heat radiated through window glass; promotes energy savings.

Header A structural member that forms the top of a window, door, or other opening to provide framing support.

Jamb The inside face of the rough opening of a window or door.

Lintel Horizontal members that span a door opening; may be structural or solely decorative.

Miter A joint in which the ends of two pieces of wood are cut at equal angles (typically 45 degrees) to form a corner.

Muntins Strips that separate window panes. On older windows, muntins hold the glass in place; on newer windows, they are often solely decorative.

On center A point of reference designating the distance between the centers of regularly spaced holes, or such parts as studs in a wall.

Paint-grade wood Wood with minor flaws, like differences in grain or color, that will be hidden by a coat of paint.

Pediment Decorative millwork set above an exterior door.

Plumb Vertically straight, in relation to horizontally level surface.

Prehung door A door that is delivered from the factory already hung in its jambs so that it need only be attached to the doorway.

Rafter A structural member that supports a pitched roof.

Rails The horizontal framing members at the top and bottom of a door; a center rail may also be used.

Sash The framework into which window glass is set. Double-hung windows have an upper and a lower sash.

Self-flashing skylight A skylight with integral flashing that does not require a curb. It is attached directly to the roof.

Shims Thin wood wedges used for tightening the fit between pieces, such as filling the gap between the window and sill when installing a window.

Single-glazed window A window with a single pane of glass held in place with glazing putty; single glazing is not energy-efficient.

Split jamb An adjustable door jamb found on some prehung units; easily adjusts to fit walls of various thicknesses.

Stain grade wood High quality wood that will not show flaws when treated with a transparent or semi-transparent finish.

Step flashing Multiple courses of galvanized metal or copper flashing installed in an overlapping fashion over a skylight curb.

Stiles The vertical framing members on each side of a door; referred to individually as the lock stile and hinge stile.

Stool The piece of window trim that provides a stop for the lower sash and extends the sill into the room.

Stops Narrow strips of wood nailed to the head and side jambs to prevent a door from swinging too far when it closes. Also keep window sash in line.

Strike plate A metal strip mortised into the side jamb to accept the latch on the lock side of a door.

Stud Vertical member of a frame wall, usually placed at either end and every 16 inches on center to facilitate covering with wallboard or paneling.

Threshold A wood or aluminum strip used on the bottom of doors to cover the gap between the sill and the floor; not often used on interior doors.

Toenail To nail two pieces of wood together by driving nails at an angle through the edge of one into the other.

Transom A horizontal window that is placed directly above an exterior door.